© Copyright 2020 - All rights reserved.

The content contained within this book may not be reproduced, duplicated or transmitted without direct written permission from the author or the publisher.

Under no circumstances will any blame or legal responsibility be held against the publisher, or author, for any damages, reparation, or monetary loss due to the information contained within this book, either directly or indirectly.

Legal Notice:

This book is copyright protected. It is only for personal use. You cannot amend, distribute, sell, use, quote or paraphrase any part, or the content within this book, without the consent of the author or publisher.

Disclaimer Notice:

Please note the information contained within this document is for educational and entertainment purposes only. All effort has been executed to present accurate, up to date, reliable, complete information. No warranties of any kind are declared or implied. Readers acknowledge that the author is not engaged in the rendering of legal, financial, medical or professional advice. The content within this book has been derived from various sources. Please consult a licensed professional before attempting any techniques outlined in this book.

By reading this document, the reader agrees that under no circumstances is the author responsible for any losses, direct or indirect, that are incurred as a result of the use of the information contained within this document, including, but not limited to, errors, omissions, or inaccuracies.

Table of Contents

Foreword 5

Introduction 6

Chapter 1: Soups and Salad for Your Soul 8

Thai Prawn Salad (Pla Gung) 8

Sesame Garlic Dressing Thai Salad 9

Crunchy Thai Salad With Peanut Dressing 10

Thai Red Curry Noodle Soup 11

Refreshing Cucumber Soup 12

Coconut Chicken Soup (Tom Ka Gai) 13

Thai Chicken Noodle Soup 14

Tom Yum Koon Soup 15

Exotic Thai Pumpkin Soup 16

Hot and Sour Tom Yum Soup with Shrimp (Tom Yum Goong) 17

Chapter 2: Thai Dishes from The Sea 18

Thai Pumpkin Seafood Stew 18

Authentic Seafood Platter (Yam Talay) 19

Crispy Fluffy Fish And Mango (Yam Pla Dook Foo) 21

Tamarind And Prawns (Goong Ma Kham) 23

Thai Steamed Mussels 24

Sardines And Lemongrass 25

Garlic And Pepper Shrimp 26

Fine Thai Tilapia Dish 27

King Prawn And Banana Salsa 28

Crispy Wonton-Wrapped Shrimp Rolls (Goong Gra Bok) 29

Chapter 3: Exotic Thai Red Meat Dishes 30

Thai Beef With Chilies And Basil (Phat Bai Horapha) 30

Perfect Pork Dumplings (Khanom Jeeb) 32

Drunken Pork Stir Fry (Pad Kee Mao) 34

Thai Pork Kabob (Pork Satay) 35

Thai Waterfall Beef (Waterfall Dish) 36

Fresh Thai Beef And Peanut Butter Dish 38

Thai Mustard Lamb Cutlets 39

Spiced Beef And Broccoli 40

Thai Fried Basil With Pork (Pad Krapow) 41

Thai Minced Pork Dish (Laab) 42

Chapter 4: Warm and Desirable Chicken Delights 43

Tasty Thai Garlic Chicken Breast 43

Lovely Fried Chicken (Gai Tod) 44

Creamy Chicken Coconut Dish (Chicken Khao Soi) 45

Authentic Chicken Fried Rice (Khao Pad) 46

Classic Thick Noodle With Chicken (Pad See Ew) 47

Perfect Thai Chicken Balls 49

Fine Chieken Massaman Curry (Matasaman Curry) 50

Thai Chicken Cashew Meal (Kai Med Ma Muang) 51
Thai Pineapple Chicken Curry 52
Chicken Satay 53

Chapter 5: Exquisite and Exciting Thai Curries 54

Authentic Green Curry Prawn 54
Thai Monkfish Curry 55
Thai Potato Yellow Curry 56
Pork Red Curry With Squash (Gaeng Daeng Sai Fak Thong Lae Moo) 57
Traditional Coconut Shrimp Curry 58
Thai Broccoli And Chickpea Curry 59
Authentic Green Curry (Gaeng Keow Wan Gai) . 60
Curried Coconut Chicken 61
Exciting Peanut Shrimp Curry 62
Panang Curry 63

Chapter 6: Inspiring Thai Veggie Delights 65

Stir-Fried Baby Mushrooms 65
Stir-Fried Bok Choy And Sesame 66
Cool Stir-Fried Vegetable (Pad Pak Ruammit) 67
Lovely Morning Glory Stir Fry (Pad Pak Boong) 68
Thai Stir-Fried Pumpkin Meal (Pad Fuk Thong) . 70
Awesome Thai Banana Custard 71
Delicious Mango Rice Pudding (Kao Niew Ma Muang) 72
A Fruity Bowl 73
Hearty Banana Fries 74
Green Papaya Mix (Som Tum) 75

Chapter 7: Amazing Rice Companions 76

Awesome Ginger Chicken With Jasmine Rice 76
Original Thai Omelet (Kai Jeow) 77
Traditional Thai Rice Pudding 78
Sweet And Spicy Coconut Mango Rice 79
Coconut Black Beans 80
Tom Yum Fried Rice with Shrimp (Khao Pad Tom Yum) 81
Green Curry Fried Rice (Khao Pad Gaeng Kiew Wan) 82
Pineapple Fried Rice with Curry Powder and Shrimp (Khao Pad Sapparot) 83
Coconut Rice (Khao Mun Gati) 85
Fresh Spring Rolls (Poh Piah Sod) 86

Chapter 8: Beautiful Noodle Based Recipes 87

The Original Noodle Soup (Guawy Teow) . 87
Thai Peanut Butter Noodles 89
Sukothai Pad Thai 90
Thai-Style Stir-Fried Macaroni (Pad Macaroni) ... 91
Pad Thai 93

Chapter 9: Refreshing Drinks 95

Refreshing Thai Iced Tea (Cha Yen) 95
Lovely Pink Milk (Thai Nom Yen) 96
Awesome Thai Bubble Tea (Boba Tea) 97
Simple Lemongrass Drink 98
Authentic Iced Coffee (Oliang) 99

Conclusion 100

Foreword

Crafting and designing a cookbook that explores the wonderful flavors of Thai cuisine isn't an easy task. Thai dishes are mostly made of a pretty complex array of ingredients that seems to mix all together to give an explosion of flavor with every bite! Just a single missing ingredient could drastically alter the flavor and create something unappealing and disappointing.

I strongly believe that the author of this book is himself a pretty strong and experience Homechef because all of the recipes in this book are fool-proof and written to perfection. While I wasn't able to try all of them, the ones I did indeed give me a taste of the most authentic Thai tradition there is.

The recipes of this book work on many levels to perfectly capture the magical essence that makes Thai cuisine so special and delicate!

After going through so many cookbooks myself and trying to find out the perfect one that fully encapsulates Thai in its entirety, I think I found the one that I love. And that is the reason why I dedicate my time to writing a foreword for this particular book.

While trying some of the most classic and traditional Thai recipes available in this book, my husband instantly became irresistible to my cooking. My kids seem to love it.

I thank the author for producing such an amazing compilation. I hope to see more similar books in the future!

The strength of a successful cookbook lies in its ability to convey expert information to beginners in easily digestible chunks. They, like real cookbooks, are intended for people who might understand the theory or fundamentals of the challenge but lack the expertise and experience that an expert steeped in the technology would have. The cookbook encourages readers to practice and participate in expert practices to correctly teach them how to do the trade tricks.

Hopefully, this book will do the same for people who are just getting started on their first journey towards becoming a Thai culinary expert and help Homechefs, both novice and advanced alike.

Alisha Patel

Sous Chef at Western Cuisine, Dhaka

Introduction

Thai cuisine has a very infamous reputation for being extremely spicy! However, the reality is far from it.

Thai foods actually represent a very interesting and delicate balance between a multitude of flavors that beautifully blends the like of sourness, spiciness, saltiness, sweetness, and bitterness to create a carnival of flavors in your taste buds.

These flavors work to complement each other and create an immaculate meal that boasts a wide array of complex and mouthwatering flavor profiles that can easily hypnotize anyone who is having Thai.

In fact, a very well-known author and chef, Thompson, has creatively expressed his thoughts regarding Thai cuisine by saying that "Thai is such a cuisine that can be easily distinguished even from its nearest neighbors it terms flavors."

The ever-increasing number of Thai restaurants is a testament to Thai food's success, as more people remember the delicious mouth-tingling delights of authentic Thai cuisine.

Thai (Tai) people were originally refugees from southwest China who settled in the north and then moved south, establishing capitals with romantic names like Sukhothai ("Dawn of Happiness"), Ayutthaya ("Unassailable"), and then Bangkok ("City of Angels") at the end of the eighteenth century. As they moved south, they discovered that the fertile central plains and abundant rainfall were ideal for high-quality paddy fields, which is why the region is known as Southeast Asia's rice bowl.

As they moved south, they discovered that the fertile central plains and abundant rainfall were ideal for high-quality paddy fields, which is why the region is known as Southeast Asia's rice bowl.

Thailand is about the size of France and has a population of about 60 million people. Its immediate neighbors are Myanmar, Laos, Cambodia, and Malaysia. Many ingredients are similar to each cuisine but are often used in entirely different cooking methods due to trade between these and other countries in the region, conveniently illustrating the argument that food has no borders or boundaries. While regional cooking exists in Thailand, Thai restaurants will typically prepare and serve well-known dishes that they know their customers will enjoy.

Thai cuisine's evolution has been a long and subtle phase, with historical and culinary influences from China. Thais adopted dry spices — coriander, cumin, nutmeg, cloves, and turmeric — from Arab and Indian traders, as used in Thai Mussaman Curry (see page 98). This added a new dimension to the work of the royal household's talented chefs, which gradually evolved into one of the world's most thrilling cuisines. The chilli, which was carried east by the Portuguese, was perhaps the most important import. Its place in Thai cooking is undeniable, but it is the clever way the various flavors are married together to distinguish Thai cuisine. Threads of Indian cuisine can also be found in Thai cuisine's rich tapestry. The wet spice pastes are reminiscent of southern Indian masalas, which invariably contain the three Cs of oriental cooking: coconut, chili, and coriander/cilantro.

Thai food's three main draws are its flavors, textures, and aromas. Red and green hot bird's eye chillies; creamy coconut; coriander/cilantro (roots, stalks, and leaves); basil leaves, with their aniseed aroma; heavenly lemon grass; pine-like galangal (Kha); torn lime leaves (just smell the citrus fragrance); limes for juice or wedges to squeeze over prepared dishes; pungent kapi (fermented shrimp paste), which has no fishy taste but gi Crisp green vegetables and unripe fruits for salads, such as green mango, meltingly tender deep-fried fish and curried meats, and juicy, simply prepared oriental fruits, such as mangosteens and lychees, are among the textures. The aroma of lemon grass and lime leaves, or the scent of curry paste mixed into coconut milk, is enough to whet the appetite.

A passion for food is a never-ending journey of discovery. There is always something different around the corner. With the popularity of Thai cuisine, the ingredients are becoming more readily available, whether in supermarkets or corner shops, so you, too, can cook authentic Thai food with the aid of these recipes.

This book aims. All the very best and top Thai recipes are included in this book and much more!

Chapter 1: Soups and Salad for Your Soul

Thai Prawn Salad (Pla Gung)

Prep Time: 10 minutes.

Cook Time: 5-6 minutes.

Serves: 4

Ingredients:

- 1 pound prawn tails
- 3 c. water
- 2 tbsp Lemon grass, coarsely chopped
- 1 tablespoon lime leaves, coarsely chopped
- 1 tablespoon coriander leaves, coarsely chopped
- 2 tablespoons lime juice
- 2 teaspoon palm sugar
- 1 tsp finely chopped garlic
- 1 teaspoon ginger, finely chopped
- 1/2 teaspoon ground black pepper
- 1/2 cup sliced green onions
- Mint leaves, 1/2 cup

Preparation:

1. Bring a pot of water to a boil, then add the lemon grass, lime leaves, and coriander. Cook for 5 minutes.
2. Cook for 1 minute after adding the prawns. Remove the item and clean it under cold water.
3. In a mixing bowl, combine lime juice, palm sugar, garlic, ginger, and black pepper. To dissolve the sugar, combine all of the ingredients.
4. Toss the prawns in the dressing to coat. Toss in the green onions and mint leaves.
5. Serve and enjoy!

Serving Suggestion: Serve over a bed of rice; you can go for sticky rice, jasmine rice, or any other rice appropriate for Thai cuisine.

Variation Tip: Add Banana Blossom during or after cooking for an additional flavorful punch.

Nutritional Information Per Serving:

Calories 251 | Fat 4g | Sodium 1196mg | Carbs 41g | Fiber 2g | Sugar 18g | Protein 15g

Sesame Garlic Dressing Thai Salad

Prep Time: 15 minutes.
Cook Time: 20 minutes.
Serves: 4

Ingredients:

To make the dressing:

- a third of a cup of canola oil
- 3 garlic cloves, peeled
- 3 tbsp. low sodium soy sauce
- 2 teaspoons water
- 2 tbsp distilled white vinegar
- 2 teaspoons honey
- 1 tbsp sesame seed oil
- 1 tbsp lemon grass paste (ginger would also work)
- a dash of lime juice

To make the salad:

- 16 ounces shelled frozen edamame
- 5–6 cups kale (baby)
- 3 medium carrots
- 2 red bell peppers (1 red, 1 yellow)
- 1 cup cilantro stems
- three green onions
- 3/4 cup cashews (Trader Joe's Thai Lime and Chili Cashews are fantastic if you can find them)

Preparation:

1. In a food processor, combine all of the dressing ingredients and puree until smooth. Taste and customize to suit your tastes. Transfer to a dressing jar and rinse the food processor for later use.
2. Boil the edamame for 3-5 minutes in a pot of boiling water. Enable to cool after draining. Meanwhile, thinly slice or shred the kale, carrots, peppers, cilantro leaves, and green onions.
3. In a food processor, pulse the cooked edamame 5 times to get a minced texture. Transfer to a bowl and do the same with the cashews. Toss together the kale, carrots, peppers, cilantro, green onions, edamame, and cashews. Drizzle with the dressing, throw a few times and serve right away.

Serving Suggestion: Serve over a bed of rice; you can go for sticky rice, jasmine rice, or any other rice appropriate for Thai cuisine.

Variation Tip: Add Banana Blossom during or after cooking for an additional flavorful punch.

Nutritional Information Per Serving:

Calories 86 | Fat 6g | Sodium 443mg | Carbs 6g | Fiber 1g | Sugar 2g | Protein 4g

Crunchy Thai Salad With Peanut Dressing

Prep Time: 30 minutes.
Cook Time: Nil
Serves: 4

Ingredients:
TO GO WITH THE THAI PEANUT DRESSING

- 1 tablespoon smooth peanut butter
- 2 tbsp rice vinegar, unseasoned
- 2 tbsp fresh lime juice (from one lime)
- three tbsp vegetable oil
- 1 teaspoon soy sauce (use gluten-free if needed)
- 2 teaspoons honey
- 2 1/2 teaspoons sugar
- 2 cloves garlic, finely chopped
- 1-inch square fresh ginger slice, peeled and roughly chopped
- 1 teaspoon sea salt
- a quarter teaspoon crushed red pepper flakes
- 2 tbsp cilantro leaves, new

TO MAKE THE SALAD

- 4 cups Napa cabbage chopped or shredded coleslaw mix (I like to toss in a little shredded red cabbage for color)
- 1 cup shredded carrots, prepared
- 1 red bell pepper, thinly sliced and diced into bite-sized pieces
- 1 small English cucumber, halved, seeded, and thinly sliced
- 1 cup edamame, cooked and shelled
- 2 thinly sliced medium scallions
- 1/2 cup chopped fresh cilantro, loosely packed

Preparation:
1. In a blender, combine all of the dressing ingredients except the cilantro and process until fully smooth. Add the cilantro and pulse for a few seconds or until it is finely chopped. Place in the refrigerator until ready to eat.
2. To make the salad, toss together all of the ingredients in a big mixing bowl. If serving immediately, drizzle the peanut dressing over the top and toss; otherwise, serve the dressing on the side to prevent the salad from being soggy

Serving Suggestion: Serve over a bed of rice; you can go for sticky rice, jasmine rice, or any other rice appropriate for Thai cuisine.
Variation Tip: Add Cilantro/Coriander/Oyster Sauce during or after cooking for an additional flavorful punch.
Nutritional Information Per Serving:
Calories 782 | Fat 36g |Sodium 2095mg | Carbs 67g | Fiber 10g | Sugar 6g | Protein 56g

Thai Red Curry Noodle Soup

Prep Time: 15 minutes.
Cook Time: 20 minutes.
Serves: 4

Ingredients:

- 1 tablespoon of olive oil
- 1 pound boneless, skinless chicken breast, cut into 1-inch chunks
- To taste, season with kosher salt and freshly ground black pepper.
- 3 minced garlic cloves
- 1 diced red bell pepper
- 1 diced onion
- 3 tbsp of red curry paste
- 1 tbsp ginger, freshly grated
- 6 cups chicken broth (low sodium)
- 1 can (13.5 oz.) coconut milk
- 1/2 box (8 oz.) rice noodles
- 1 teaspoon fish sauce
- 2 tablespoons brown sugar

- 3 thinly sliced green onions
- 1/2 cup clean cilantro leaves, chopped
- 1/4 cup organic basil leaves, chopped
- 2 tbsp lime juice, freshly squeezed

Preparation:

1. In a big stockpot or Dutch oven, heat the olive oil over medium heat. Season the chicken to taste with salt and pepper. Cook the chicken in the stockpot until golden, about 2-3 minutes; set aside.
2. Mix in the garlic, bell pepper, and onion. Cook, stirring periodically, until the vegetables are tender, around 3-4 minutes.
3. Stir in the red curry paste and ginger for around 1 minute, or until fragrant.
4. Scrape any browned bits from the bottom of the pot and stir in the chicken broth and coconut milk.
5. Add the chicken and mix well. Bring to a boil; reduce heat and cook, stirring periodically, for 10 minutes, or until reduced.
6. Stir in the rice noodles, fish sauce, and brown sugar for about 5 minutes, or until the noodles are soft.
7. Remove from heat; stir in green onions, cilantro, basil, and lime juice; season to taste with salt and pepper.
8. Serve right away

Serving Suggestion: Add some crumbled noodles on top; it will give an extra crunch

Variation Tip: Add Coriander/Oyster Sauce during or after cooking for an additional flavorful punch.

Nutritional Information Per Serving:

Calories 480 | Fat 10g | Sodium 1553mg | Carbs 72g | Fiber 15g | Sugar 15g | Protein 24g

Refreshing Cucumber Soup

Prep Time: 15 minutes.
Cook Time: 30 minutes.
Serves: 4

Ingredients:

- 2 tablespoons butter
- 2 tablespoons green onion, sliced
- 3 cucumbers, chopped
- 1/3 cup red wine vinegar
- 1-quart chicken broth
- 2 cups water
- 3 hot chicle pepper, minced and seeded
- 3 tablespoons fresh parsley, chopped
- 1 tablespoon fresh cilantro, chopped
- 1 tablespoon fish sauce
- 1 teaspoon soy sauce
- Salt as needed
- Pepper as needed
- ½ cup sour cream

Preparation:

1. Take a deep pan and place it over medium heat
2. Add butter and allow it to heat up
3. Add green onions and cook them until tender
4. Stir in vinegar, cucumber, chicken broth, chile peppers, water, parsley, lemon grass, cilantro, garlic, soy sauce, fish sauce, ginger
5. Season with some salt and pepper
6. Simmer it over medium heat until the cucumbers are tender for about 20 minutes
7. Stir in sour cream and simmer for 10 minutes more
8. Enjoy!

Serving Suggestion: If possible, add a bit of cream

Variation Tip: Add shredded coconut on top.

Nutritional Information Per Serving:
Calories 135 | Fat 8g | Sodium 655mg | Carbs 11g | Fiber 2g | Sugar 8g | Protein 5g

Coconut Chicken Soup (Tom Ka Gai)

Prep Time: 15 minutes.
Cook Time: 20 minutes.
Serves: 4

Ingredients:

- ¾ pound of boneless chicken meat
- 3 tablespoon of vegetable oil
- 2 cans of 14-ounce coconut milk
- 2 tablespoon of fresh ginger root, minced
- 4 tablespoon of fish sauce
- ¼ cup of fresh lime juice
- ¼ cup of fresh lime juice
- ¼ teaspoon of cayenne pepper
- ½ teaspoon of ground turmeric
- 2 tablespoons of green onion, sliced
- 1 tablespoon of fresh cilantro, chopped

Preparation:

1. Cut up your chicken into strips
2. Take a skillet and place it over medium heat, add oil, and heat it up
3. Add the chicken strips and Sauté them for about 2-3 minutes
4. Take a pot and bring the coconut milk and water to a boil
5. Lower down the heat to low
6. Add ginger, lime juice, fish sauce, turmeric, and cayenne powder
7. Simmer the chicken for about 10-15 minutes
8. Sprinkle it with a bit of cilantro and scallions
9. Serve hot!

Serving Suggestion: If possible, add a bit of cream on top before serving, and some mint on top

Variation Tip: Add Banana Blossom/Basil during or after cooking for an additional flavorful punch.

Nutritional Information Per Serving:

Calories 303 | Fat 21g |Sodium 662mg | Carbs 16g | Fiber 1g | Sugar 7g | Protein 15g

Thai Chicken Noodle Soup

Prep Time: 15 minutes.
Cook Time: 20 minutes.
Serves: 4

Ingredients:

- 4 ounces of dry Chinese noodles
- 1 can of 14.5 ounces of chicken broth
- 6 shitake mushrooms, sliced
- 2 green onions, chopped
- 1 skinless and boneless chicken breast half
- 2 eggs

Preparation:

1. Take a bowl of water and bring it to a boil
2. Stir in noodles and cook until Al Dente for about 8-10 minutes
3. Drain the noodles and divide them into two serving bowls
4. Take a medium-sized saucepan and place it over medium heat
5. Add chicken broth and bring it to a boil
6. Add green onions and mushrooms
7. Cut up the chicken into bite-sized portions and stir it into the broth
8. Once the broth comes to a boil, crack in the eggs
9. Keep cooking for about 10 minutes until the chickens are no longer pink, and the eggs are cooked
10. Pour the chicken soup over the noodle bowls
11. Enjoy!

Serving Suggestion: Add some crunchy noodle on top for additional crunch

Variation Tip: Add Cilantro/Coriander/Oyster Sauce during or after cooking for an additional flavorful punch.

Nutritional Information Per Serving:

Calories 902 | Fat 56g |Sodium 1455mg | Carbs 29g | Fiber 5g | Sugar 5g | Protein 68g

Tom Yum Koon Soup

Prep Time: 15 minutes.
Cook Time: 40 minutes.
Serves: 4

Ingredients:

- ½ a pound of medium-sized peeled and deveined shrimp
- 12 mushrooms, halved
- 1 can of 4.5 ounces of drained mushrooms
- 4 cups of water
- 2 lemon grass
- 4 kaffir lime leaves
- 4 slices of galangal
- 4 chile Padi
- 1 and a ½ tablespoon of fish sauce
- 1 and a ½ juice limes
- 1 teaspoon of white sugar

- 1 teaspoon of hot Chile paste
- 1 tablespoon of tom yum sour paste

Preparation:

1. Trim the lemongrass and cut them up into matchstick-size portions
2. Take a bowl and place it over medium-high heat
3. Add shrimp heads and shells to water
4. Cook for about 20 minutes
5. Remove the heat
6. Soak the head and shells for about 20 minutes, discard them
7. Trim the lemongrass into matchstick portions
8. Take a pot and add lemon grass, stock, kaffir lime leaves, chili Padi, lime juice, fish sauce, galangal, sugar, and Chili paste
9. Bring it to a boil and allow it to boil for 5 minutes
10. Add shrimps and mushrooms
11. Cook for 10 minutes more
12. Garnish with some coriander leaves
13. Enjoy!

Serving Suggestion: Serve over a bed of rice; you can go for sticky rice, jasmine rice, or any other rice appropriate for Thai cuisine.

Variation Tip: Add Banana Blossom /Oyster Sauce during or after cooking for an additional flavorful punch.

Nutritional Information Per Serving:

Calories 260 | Fat 9g |Sodium 1439mg | Carbs 18g | Fiber 3g | Sugar 3g | Protein 29g

Exotic Thai Pumpkin Soup

Prep Time: 10 minutes.
Cook Time: 15 minutes.
Serves: 4

Ingredients:

- 1 tablespoon of vegetable oil
- 1 tablespoon of butter
- 1 chopped garlic clove
- 4 chopped shallots
- 2 small-sized fresh red chili pepper chopped up
- 1 tablespoon of chopped lemon grass
- 2 and 1/8 cups of chicken stock
- 4 cups of peeled and diced pumpkin
- 1 and a ½ cups of unsweetened coconut milk
- 1 bunch of fresh basil leaves

Preparation:

1. Take a medium-sized saucepan and place it over low heat
2. Add oil and heat it up
3. Add butter and melt
4. Add garlic, chiles, shallots, lemongrass, and stir until fragrant
5. Stir in chicken stock, pumpkin, and coconut milk
6. Bring the mixture to a boil
7. Cook until the pumpkin is tender
8. Take a blender and blend the sup in batches until a smooth soup form
9. Serve the soup with some basil leaves!

Serving Suggestion: Add a bit of cream before serving for added flavor

Variation Tip: Add Cilantro/Coriander/Oyster Sauce during or after cooking for an additional flavorful punch.

Nutritional Information Per Serving:

Calories 268 | Fat 17g | Sodium 81mg | Carbs 29g | Fiber 2g | Sugar 14g | Protein 5g

Hot and Sour Tom Yum Soup with Shrimp (Tom Yum Goong)

Prep Time: 10 minutes.
Cook Time: 5 minutes.
Serves: 4

Ingredients:

- 4 cups water or Basic Thai Chicken Stock
- 6 (1/8-inch-thick) slices unpeeled fresh galangal, bruised with the butt of a chef's knife, optional
- 3 lemongrass stalks (bottom 3 inches only), bruised with the flat side of a chef's knife
- 2 fresh kaffir lime leaves, optional
- 2 tablespoons Roasted Chili Paste
- 3 tablespoons fish sauce
- 1 cup fresh button mushrooms cut into ¼-inch slices, or canned straw mushrooms, drained and halved or left whole
- 12 large raw shrimp, deveined, peeled, or impeded, as you prefer; if removing the shell, leave tails on for a nicer presentation
- ¼ cup lime juice, freshly squeezed
- 1 or 2 fresh red Thai bird's-eye chiles, stemmed, seeded, and each thinly sliced lengthwise into 4 strips, optional
- ¼ cup fresh cilantro leaves, for serving

Preparation:

1. Take a medium saucepan and add water, lemongrass, and kaffir lime leaves into it.
2. Cover and bring just to a boil over high heat.
3. Turn the heat to low and simmer for 5 minutes.
4. Remove and discard lemongrass and lime leaves.
5. Stir in the chili paste.
6. Add the mushrooms and simmer for 1 minute.
7. Then add the shrimp and simmer for 1 minute more.
8. Remove from the heat and stir in the lime juice and chiles.
9. Adjust the seasoning, as needed, with additional fish sauce or lime juice.
10. Take a small bowl and sprinkle with cilantro on top.
11. Serve and enjoy!

Serving Suggestion: Serve over a bed of rice; you can go for sticky rice, jasmine rice, or any other rice appropriate for Thai cuisine.

Variation Tip: Add Banana Blossom/Basil/Chili Peppers during or after cooking for an additional flavorful punch.

Nutritional Information Per Serving:
Calories 167 | Fat 6g | Sodium 1429mg | Carbs 16g | Fiber 3g | Sugar 5g | Protein 14g

Chapter 2: Thai Dishes from The Sea

Thai Pumpkin Seafood Stew

Prep Time: 15 minutes.
Cook Time: 35 minutes.
Serves: 4

Ingredients:

- 1 and ½ tablespoons fresh galangal, chopped
- 1 teaspoon lime zest
- 1 small kabocha squash
- 32 medium-sized mussels, fresh
- 1 pound shrimp
- 16 thai leaves
- 1 can coconut milk
- 1 tablespoon lemongrass, minced
- 4 garlic cloves, roughly chopped
- 32 medium clams, fresh
- 1 and ½ pounds fresh salmon
- 2 tablespoon coconut oil
- Pepper to taste

Preparation:

1. Add coconut milk, lemongrass, galangal, garlic, lime leaves in a small-sized saucepan, bring to a boil.
2. Let it simmer for 25 minutes.
3. Strain mixture through a fine sieve into the large soup pot and bring to a simmer.
4. Add oil to a pan and heat up; add Kabocha squash.
5. Season with salt and pepper, Sauté for 5 minutes.
6. Add mix to coconut mix.
7. Heat oil in a pan and add fish shrimp, season with salt and pepper, cook for 4 minutes.
8. Add mixture to coconut milk mix alongside clams and mussels.
9. Simmer for 8 minutes, garnish with basil and enjoy!

Serving Suggestion: Serve with some bread or fried rice

Variation Tip: Add Banana Blossom/Coriander/Oyster Sauce during or after cooking for an additional flavorful punch.

Nutritional Information Per Serving:

Calories 434 | Fat 18g | Sodium 741mg | Carbs 24g | Fiber 4 g | Sugar 6g | Protein 38g

Authentic Seafood Platter (Yam Talay)

Prep Time: 15 minutes.
Cook Time: 10-15 minutes.
Serves: 4

Ingredients:

For Seafood

- 24 small mussels
- 1 tablespoon table salt
- 3/4 pound medium (51 to 60 per lb.) new peeled and deveined shrimp
- 1/2 pound washed squid, sliced crosswise into 1/4-inch circles, tentacles cut in half if wide
- half pound sea scallops or bay scallops
- 1/4 pound jumbo lump crabmeat, fresh or pasteurized

To make the dressing:

- 6 tablespoons new lime juice (from 2 limes)
- 4 1/2 tablespoons fish sauce
- 1 1/2 tablespoons granulated sugar
- 2 teaspoons finely chopped unseeded fresh hot green chiles (such as serrano or jalapeno)
- 2 tablespoons finely chopped garlic (2 medium cloves)

To make the salad:

- 2 cups rinsed and spun-dry bite-size Boston lettuce (1 large head)
- 3 tablespoons thinly sliced shallot (1 large)
- 1/3 cup scallions, thinly sliced (4 to 5, white and green parts)
- 1/4 cup fresh cilantro, coarsely chopped
- 1/4 cup new mint, coarsely chopped
- 1/2 cup sliced English cucumber (cut cucumber in half lengthwise and slice into 1/4-inch thick half-moons)
- 1/2 cup cherry or grape tomatoes, halved

Preparation:

1. Scrub the mussels thoroughly under running water and remove any "beards." Any mussels that do not close tightly when tapped on the counter should be discarded. In a medium saucepan, place closed mussels. Pour in around 1/2 cup water, just enough to reach the bottom of the pan by 1/4 inch. Set over high heat, covered. Bring to a boil and cook for 1 to 2 minutes, or until the shells have opened. Remove from the sun, switch to a tray, and leave to cool before you can handle it. Throw away those that haven't been opened. Place the cooked mussels in a medium bowl and remove the shells and cooking liquid.

2. Bring a 3-quart saucepan of water to a boil over high heat to cook the remaining seafood. Return the water to a boil after adding the salt. Pour the shrimp into the boiling water and cook for 2 minutes, or until the largest one

is pink on the outside, opaque on the inside, and only cooked through. The water cannot come back to a boil until it is done. Scoop them out with a slotted spoon and place them in the same bowl as the mussels.

3. After the water returns to a rolling boil, add the squid and cook for around 1 minute, or until they become firm and the rings turn bright white. Scoop them out and toss them in with the shrimp and mussels in the tub.

4. When the water returns to a boil, cook the scallops for 1 to 2 minutes for bay scallops and 2 to 3 minutes for sea scallops, or until just cooked through and no longer translucent inside. Scoop them out and place them in the bowl as well (if using sea scallops, you may want to halve or quarter them first).

5. Add the lump crabmeat chunks to the seafood dish. Set the seafood aside on the counter as you make the dressing and other salad ingredients.

To make the dressing and salad

1. Combine the lime juice, fish sauce, sugar, chiles, and garlic in a medium-large mixing bowl. Stir to remove the sugar and thoroughly mix everything. Place aside.

2. Assemble the salad as follows:

3. Arrange the lettuce as a bed for the seafood on a big serving platter or individual serving plates.

4. Place the cooked seafood in the bowl with the lime-juice dressing. Add the shallots and gently toss everything together with your hands or a wooden spoon.

5. Mix in the scallions, cilantro, and mint until well combined. Using a slotted spoon, transfer the seafood to the platter or serving plates. Toss the cucumber and tomato in the remaining dressing in the tub, then scatter over the seafood.

6. Drizzle any leftover dressing from the bowl over the salad, paying particular attention to any lettuce that hasn't been covered by the seafood. Serve right away

Serving Suggestion: Serve over a bed of rice; you can go for sticky rice, jasmine rice, or any other rice appropriate for Thai cuisine.

Variation Tip: Add /Coriander/Oyster Sauce during or after cooking for an additional flavorful punch.

Nutritional Information Per Serving:

Calories 403 | Fat 30g |Sodium 1387mg | Carbs 4g | Fiber 1g | Sugar 1g | Protein 28g

Crispy Fluffy Fish And Mango (Yam Pla Dook Foo)

Prep Time: 15 minutes.
Cook Time: 20 minutes.
Serves: 4

Ingredients:

For the Mango Salad

- To taste, Thai chilies
- 2 tbsp palm sugar, finely chopped
- 2 tablespoons fish sauce
- 2 tablespoons lime juice
- 12 thinly sliced shallot
- 1 tbsp dried shrimp, diced 1 julienned sour green mango (see note)
- 2 tbsp cilantro, chopped

For Fish

- ½ pound of any kind of fish meat
- 1 teaspoon soy sauce or a pinch of salt
- 3 tablespoons roasted peanuts
- frying oil

Preparation:

1. Season the fish with soy sauce or salt and steam for 5 minutes or until the meat is completely cooked. If you don't want to steam the fish, you can cook it in whatever way you want as long as you don't get a browned crispy crust on it (poach, bake, even stir-fry in a pan on low heat). When done, allow the fish to cool so you can handle it more easily.
2. Make the mango salad while the fish is cooking and cooling. Pound the Thai chilies in a mortar until there are no more large chunks (chili skin is fine), then add the palm sugar and mash until it's a muddy paste. Swirl in the fish sauce and lime juice until the sugar is fully dissolved. Transfer to a mixing bowl and add the dried shrimp, shallots, and mango. Allow setting while you cook the fish.
3. When the fish has cooled enough to treat, place it in a muslin-lined tub. Wrap the cloth around the fish, twist it to hold the fish in the cloth, and squeeze as hard as you can to get rid of as much liquid as possible (this is why you should let the fish cool; if it's too warm, you won't want to squeeze as hard!).
4. Transfer the fish to a mortar and pestle, and pound it until soft and free of chunks.
5. Heat about 1 - 1.5 inch of oil in a wok or deep pot over high heat to 400°F, and please read and observe the safety precautions above! Tip: It would be easier to fold the fish if you use a larger pot or wok for this since you will be able to get to it more quickly. Note: For the amount specified in this recipe, you can make two batches of fried fish in a 9-inch-diameter pot.
6. When the oil reaches temperature, add about half of the fish, and the oil will bubble vigorously. Push the edges of the fish in with a skimmer to clean them up, then leave the fish to fry until golden. I like to force the fish down every now and then so the top is submerged, which helps the fish brown more uniformly. When the fish is golden

brown, you can fold it over into a half circle or any shape you like, but this is not needed. Take the fish from the oil with a slotted skimmer and shake it several times to extract the oil that has become trapped inside the fish until the bubbling has slowed and the fish is golden all over. Set aside on a paper towel to drain.

7. Arrange the fish on a plate and top with roasted peanuts. Serve the mango salad alongside the tuna, garnished with chopped cilantro. With jasmine rice, serve. Have fun!

Serving Suggestion: Serve over a bed of rice; you can go for sticky rice, jasmine rice, or any other rice appropriate for Thai cuisine.

Variation Tip: Add Coriander/Oyster Sauce during or after cooking for an additional flavorful punch.

Nutritional Information Per Serving:

Calories 351 | Fat 26g | Sodium 372mg | Carbs 29g | Fiber 7g | Sugar 16g | Protein 7g

Tamarind And Prawns (Goong Ma Kham)

Prep Time: 15 minutes + marinate time.
Cook Time: 4 minutes.
Serves: 4

Ingredients:

- Coriander leaves for garnish
- 21 ounces of raw prawns, peeled and deveined
- 1 teaspoon of freshly ground black pepper
- ¼ teaspoon of crushed dried chili
- 2 tablespoon of tamarind pulp
- 1 tablespoon of light soy sauce
- ½ a teaspoon of soft brown sugar
- Just a pinch of salt
- 2 tablespoon of vegetable oil

Preparation:

1. Take a bowl and add all of the ingredients except salt, oil, and prawn; mix them well
2. Add prawns and cover them, leave them for about 30 minutes, making sure to turn them 2-3 minutes
3. Season the prawns with salt
4. Take a frying pan and place it over medium-high heat
5. Add vegetable oil and allow it to heat up
6. Add prawns and fry them for 2 minutes until both sides are dark brown
7. Garnish them with some fresh coriander leaves and serve with some cucumber slices
8. Enjoy!

Serving Suggestion: Serve over a bed of rice; you can go for sticky rice, jasmine rice, or any other rice appropriate for Thai cuisine.

Variation Tip: Add Banana Blossom/Coriander/Oyster Sauce during or after cooking for an additional flavorful punch.

Nutritional Information Per Serving:

Calories 899 | Fat 55g |Sodium 252mg | Carbs 83g | Fiber 12g | Sugar 22g | Protein 20g

Thai Steamed Mussels

Prep Time: 15 minutes.
Cook Time: 10 minutes.
Serves: 4

Ingredients:

- 5 pounds of fresh mussels, debearded and scrubbed
- ¼ cup of fresh lime juice
- 1 can of unsweetened coconut milk
- ¼ cup of dry white wine
- 1 and a ½ tablespoon of Thai red curry paste
- 1 and a ½ tablespoon garlic, minced
- 1 tablespoon of Asian fish sauce
- 1 tablespoon of white sugar
- 2 cups of chopped fresh cilantro

Preparation:

1. Take a large-sized stock pot
2. Add lime juice, coconut milk, wine, garlic, curry paste, fish sauce, and sugar
3. Stir sugar and dissolve alongside the curry paste
4. Bring it to a boil over high heat
5. Boil for about 2 minutes
6. Add mussels and cover, and cook for about 5-8 minutes
7. Remove the heat and discard any unopened mussels
8. Pour mussels and liquid into a serving dish
9. Add cilantro, and enjoy!

Serving Suggestion: Serve over a bed of rice; you can go for sticky rice, jasmine rice, or any other rice appropriate for Thai cuisine.

Variation Tip: Add Banana Blossom/Oyster Sauce during or after cooking for an additional flavorful punch.

Nutritional Information Per Serving:
Calories 439 | Fat 26g | Sodium 1269mg | Carbs 16g | Fiber 1g | Sugar 3g | Protein 32g

Sardines And Lemongrass

Prep Time: 15 minutes.
Cook Time: Nil
Serves: 4

Ingredients:

- 2 tablespoons of Thai Sweet Chile Sauce
- 1 tablespoon of lime juice
- ½ a teaspoon of kosher salt
- 1 lemon grass, tough outer leaves discarded, and the inner core thinly sliced up
- 1 can of 3 and a ¾ ounce of sardines, drained and cut up into 1-inch pieces
- 1 and a ½ cups of lightly packed torn cilantro leaves
- ½ small red onion, sliced

Preparation:

1. Take a large-sized bowl whisk in the chile sauce, lime juice, and salt
2. Mix well
3. Add cilantro, lemongrass, sardines, and red onions
4. Toss well
5. Transfer to your serving platter and enjoy!

Serving Suggestion: Serve over a bed of rice; you can go for sticky rice, jasmine rice, or any other rice appropriate for Thai cuisine.

Variation Tip: Add Oyster Sauce during or after cooking for an additional flavorful punch.

Nutritional Information Per Serving:
Calories 227 | Fat 6g | Sodium 272mg | Carbs 29g | Fiber 3g | Sugar 4g | Protein 15g

Garlic And Pepper Shrimp

Prep Time: 25 minutes.
Cook Time: 10 minutes.
Serves: 4

Ingredients:

- 2 and a ½ tablespoon of vegetable oil
- ¼ cup of water
- 1 cup of shredded cabbage
- 1 tablespoon of garlic, minced
- 8 large-sized peeled and deveined shrimp
- 2 teaspoon of crushed red pepper flakes
- 2 tablespoons of sliced onion
- 1 tablespoon of fresh cilantro, chopped
- 1 tablespoon of soy sauce

Preparation:

1. Take a metal skillet and place it over high heat
2. Add 1 tablespoon of oil and heat it up
3. Add cabbage and 1 tablespoon of water to stir fry the cabbage for 30 seconds
4. Remove your cabbage and place it on the serving platter
5. Add 1 and a ½ tablespoon of oil to the skillet and place it over high heat again
6. Add garlic and shrimp and cook until the shrimp turns pink
7. Add your onion, pepper, cilantro, water, and soy sauce to the skillet
8. Stir fry for about 10 seconds
9. Pour the mix into the cabbage and serve!

Serving Suggestion: Serve over a bed of rice; you can go for sticky rice, jasmine rice, or any other rice appropriate for Thai cuisine.

Variation Tip: Add Banana Blossom during or after cooking for an additional flavorful punch.

Nutritional Information Per Serving:

Calories 182 | Fat 6g |Sodium 436mg | Carbs 24g | Fiber 1g | Sugar 0g | Protein 7g

Fine Thai Tilapia Dish

Prep Time: 15 minutes.
Cook Time: 20 minutes.
Serves: 4

Ingredients:

- ½ a cup of coconut milk
- 6 whole almonds
- 2 tablespoons of chopped white onion
- 1 teaspoon of ground ginger
- ½ a teaspoon of ground turmeric
- 1 teaspoon of chopped fresh lemon grass
- ¼ teaspoon of salt
- 4 ounce of tilapia fillets
- Salt as needed
- Pepper as needed
- ½ a teaspoon of red pepper flakes

Preparation:

1. Take a food processor and add coconut milk, onion, almonds, ginger, lemon grass, and ¼ teaspoon of salt
2. Process well
3. Take a large-sized skillet and place it over medium-high heat
4. Season the fish fillets with salt and pepper on both sides
5. Add them to the skillet skin side up
6. Pour the pureed sauce over the fish
7. Use a spatula to coat the fish evenly
8. Sprinkle red pepper flakes
9. Lower down the heat to medium and simmer for about 15 minutes
10. Enjoy!

Serving Suggestion: Serve over a bed of rice; you can go for sticky rice, jasmine rice, or any other rice appropriate for Thai cuisine.

Variation Tip: Add Banana Blossom/Basil/Chili Peppers/Cilantro/Coriander/Oyster Sauce during or after cooking for an additional flavorful punch.

Nutritional Information Per Serving:
Calories 211 | Fat 10g |Sodium 379mg | Carbs 3g | Fiber 1g | Sugar 0g | Protein 29g

King Prawn And Banana Salsa

Prep Time: 15 minutes.
Cook Time: 5 minutes.
Serves: 4

Ingredients:

- 2 bananas, peeled and sliced
- 2 cucumbers, peeled and diced
- ½ cup fresh mint leaves
- ½ cup fresh cilantro leaves
- 1 fresh red chile pepper, sliced
- ¼ cup lime juice
- 1 tablespoon fish sauce
- 1 tablespoon brown sugar
- 1 and ½ pound tiger prawns, peeled and deveined

Preparation:

1. Take a large-sized bowl and add cucumbers, bananas, ginger, cilantro, red chile pepper, and mix everything well to prepare the Salsa
2. Take a small-sized bowl and add lime juice, fish sauce, brown sugar, and blend well until the mixture has fully dissolved
3. Thoroughly mix up your salsa
4. Take a large-sized saucepan and add a bit of lightly salted water; bring the water to a boil
5. Add your prawns into the water and cook for 3 minutes
6. Serve with your banana salsa!

Serving Suggestion: Serve over a bed of rice; you can go for sticky rice, jasmine rice, or any other rice appropriate for Thai cuisine.

Variation Tip: Add Oyster Sauce during or after cooking for an additional flavorful punch.

Nutritional Information Per Serving:
Calories 251 | Fat 4g |Sodium 1196mg | Carbs 35g | Fiber 7g | Sugar 18g | Protein 15g

Crispy Wonton-Wrapped Shrimp Rolls (Goong Gra Bok)

Prep Time: 5 minutes.

Cook Time: 5 to 10 minutes.

Serves: 4

Ingredients:

- 30 wonton wrappers
- 1 pound peeled, deveined, tail-on raw shrimp (about 30)
- Neutral oil, such as peanut or refined coconut oil, for frying
- Sweet Chili Sauce

Preparation:

1. Clean your work surface and place the wrappers.
2. Use your finger to straighten out each shrimp a bit and place it at the edge of one of the wrappers, leaving the tail off the wrapper.
3. Bring the remaining wrapper all the way over to cover the shrimp.
4. Then, use your thumbs to grab the edge on which the shrimp is lying and roll up to form a cylinder.
5. Use water at the tip of your finger to seal the wrapper.
6. Take a deep skillet over medium-high heat, heat 1 inch of oil to 375 degrees F
7. Fry the rolls in batches
8. Be careful not to overcrowd them, just until crisp and golden brown, 1 to 2 minutes.
9. Drain well on paper towels and serve with chili sauce for dipping.
10. Serve and enjoy!

Serving Suggestion: Serve them as a side with your main dishes, such as fried rice or curries

Variation Tip: Add Banana Blossom/Coriander/Oyster Sauce during or after cooking for an additional flavorful punch.

Nutritional Information Per Serving:

Calories 880 | Fat 27g |Sodium 1573mg | Carbs 114g | Fiber 4g | Sugar 2g | Protein 41g

Chapter 3: Exotic Thai Red Meat Dishes

Thai Beef With Chilies And Basil (Phat Bai Horapha)

Prep Time: 15 minutes.
Cook Time: 15 minutes.
Serves: 3

Ingredients:

- 1 pound (450g) flank steak, skirt steak, hanger steak, or flap beef, thinly sliced
- 1 tablespoon (15ml) soy sauce,
- 5 teaspoons (25ml) Asian fish sauce,
- 1 teaspoon (4g) granulated sugar
- 4 to 6 Thai bird chilies, fresh red or green, divided
- 6 medium garlic cloves, divided 1 1/2 tbsp (20g) palm sugar (see note)
- 1 small shallot, thinly sliced 4 makrut lime leaves, thinly sliced into hairs (central vein removed), plus more for garnish (see note)
- 2 tbsp (30 mL) vegetable or canola oil, divided
- 2 cups packed Thai purple basil (approximately 2 oz; 55g)
- To taste, add dried Thai chili flakes or red pepper flakes (optional)
- ¼ cups fried shallots
- Kosher salt is kosher salt.

Preparation:

1. In a mixing bowl, combine the meat, 1 teaspoon soy sauce, 2 teaspoons fish sauce, and white sugar. Toss all together and place in the refrigerator to marinate for at least 15 minutes and up to overnight.
2. Place half of the Thai chilies and garlic in a stone mortar with palm sugar. Using a pestle, grind until mostly smooth paste forms. Mash the remaining fish sauce and soy sauce in a mortar to make a sauce. Place aside. In a small bowl, finely slice the remaining garlic and chilies and mix with the shallot and lime leaves.
3. When you're ready to cook, heat 1 tablespoon oil in a wok over high heat until it begins to smoke. Cook, without moving the beef, until well seared, around 1 minute. Cook, stir, and constantly tossing until the beef is lightly cooked but still pink in spots, around 1 minute. Transfer to a big mixing bowl. Repeat with 1 tablespoon more oil and the remaining beef, moving beef to the same bowl each time. Wipe out the wok.
4. Reheat the wok over high heat and add the remaining beef and the sliced garlic/chili/makrut lime mixture. Cook, tossing, and stirring continuously, for 1 minute, or until the stir-fry is aromatic and the shallots are fully softened.
5. Cook, tossing, and stirring continuously until the sauce mixture is totally reduced in the wok. (The beef should appear moist, but there should be no liquid in the wok.) Toss in the basil right away to mix. Season with salt and

optional Thai chili or red pepper flakes to taste. Place on a serving platter. More makrut lime threads and fried shallots on top. Serve with rice right away.

Serving Suggestion: Serve over a bed of rice; you can go for sticky rice, jasmine rice, or any other rice appropriate for Thai cuisine.

Variation Tip: Add Coriander/Oyster Sauce during or after cooking for an additional flavorful punch.

Nutritional Information Per Serving:

Calories 248 | Fat 17g |Sodium 339mg | Carbs 8g | Fiber 1g | Sugar 2g | Protein 16g

Perfect Pork Dumplings (Khanom Jeeb)

Prep Time: 45 minutes.
Cook Time: 15 minutes.
Serves: 4

Ingredients:

For Garlic Oil

- 3 tbsp. vegetable oil for
- 3 garlic cloves, minced

For Wonton

- 5 whole black peppercorns
- 2 garlic cloves, peeled, salt to taste
- 2 cilantro stems, chopped
- 5 ounces pork, ground
- 5 oz. minced shrimp
- 5 water chestnut, minced
- 1 tbsp. dark soy sauce
- 1 teaspoon of white sugar
- 1 tsp. fish sauce
- 1 tbsp tapioca starch
- 1 teaspoon soy sauce (light)
- 1/2 tablespoon of salt
- 25 wonton wrappers (or as many as you need)

Sauce for dipping

- 3 tbsp rice vinegar
- 3 tbsp soy sauce (light)
- 1 teaspoon of white sugar
- 2 scallions, thinly sliced
- 1 bird's eye chile (or more as desired) (Optional)

Preparation:

1. In a small skillet over medium-low heat, heat the vegetable oil and add the minced garlic.
2. Cook until the garlic is golden brown for about 5 minutes. Remove the skillet from the heat.
3. Using a mortar and pestle, crush the peppercorns until they are powdery. Crush peeled garlic and a pinch of salt into a paste. Combine the cilantro stems with the paste.
4. In a big mixing bowl, add the paste, pork, shrimp, water chestnuts, dark soy sauce, 1 tablespoon white sugar, fish sauce, tapioca starch, light soy sauce, and 1/2 teaspoon salt. Mix well.
5. Fill each wonton wrapper with 1 to 2 teaspoons of the pork-shrimp mixture. Fold the wrapper over the filling to form a purse-like pouch, locking the edges together.

6. Fill a saucepan halfway with water to just below the bottom of a steamer insert. Get a pot of water to a boil. Cover and steam the wontons for about 10 minutes or until the filling is cooked through.
7. In a mixing bowl, combine rice vinegar, light soy sauce, 1 tablespoon white sugar, scallions, and bird's eye chile until well combined.
8. Serve Khanom Jeeb with dipping sauce and a drizzle of garlic oil on the side.

Serving Suggestion: Serve over a bed of rice; you can go for sticky rice, jasmine rice, or any other rice appropriate for Thai cuisine.

Variation Tip: Add Oyster Sauce during or after cooking for an additional flavorful punch.

Nutritional Information Per Serving:

Calories 374 | Fat 4g | Sodium 1620mg | Carbs 62g | Fiber 2g | Sugar 4g | Protein 21g

Drunken Pork Stir Fry (Pad Kee Mao)

Prep Time: 20 minutes.
Cook Time: 20 minutes.
Serves: 4

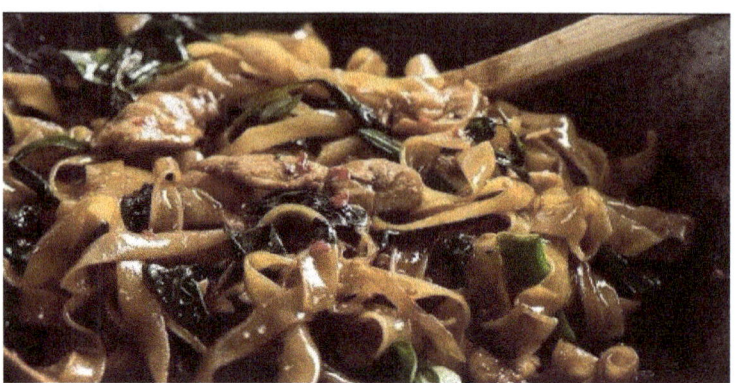

Ingredients:

- 3 1/2 ounces wide dried Thai-style rice noodles (such as Chan taboon Rice Noodles)
- 1/2 teaspoon olive oil
- 2 minced garlic cloves
- 1/2 tsp thick soy sauce
- 2 tsp of white sugar
- 1/2 teaspoon olive oil
- 2 minced garlic cloves
- 1/2 pound thinly sliced pork (any cut)
- 1 serrano pepper, minced (or more as desired)
- 1/2 teaspoon thick soy sauce 30 fresh basil leaves, chopped
- 1 teaspoon granulated sugar
- 1 teaspoon sea salt
- 1/2 cup steamed bean sprouts

Preparation:

1. Place the dry rice noodles in a cup, cover with hot water, and soak for 1 hour, or until white and softened. Drain and set aside the noodles.
2. In a wok or large skillet over low heat, heat 1 1/2 teaspoon olive oil and cook and stir 2 minced garlic cloves until brown and beginning to crisp, 2 to 3 minutes.
3. Stir in the soaked noodles, 1/2 teaspoon thick soy sauce, and 2 teaspoons sugar, and cook and stir for 3 minutes, or until the noodles have absorbed the soy sauce and turned brown. Take the noodles out of the skillet.
4. In the wok, heat the remaining 1 1/2 teaspoons olive oil over low heat; add the remaining 2 minced garlic cloves and cook until brown and beginning to crisp, 2 to 3 minutes. Stir in the pork, serrano pepper, basil, 1/2 teaspoon thick soy sauce, 1 teaspoon sugar, and salt.
5. Cook and stir for 5 minutes, or until the pork is no longer pink and the edges of the meat begin to brown. Stir in the bean sprouts and return the noodles to the wok.
6. Cook and stir for another 5 minutes, or until thoroughly cooked.

Serving Suggestion: Serve over a bed of rice; you can go for sticky rice, jasmine rice, or any other rice appropriate for Thai cuisine.

Variation Tip: Add Cilantro/Coriander/Oyster Sauce during or after cooking for an additional flavorful punch.

Nutritional Information Per Serving:

Calories 405 | Fat 20g |Sodium 94mg | Carbs 33g | Fiber 3g | Sugar 24g | Protein 22g

Thai Pork Kabob (Pork Satay)

Prep Time: 45 minutes.
Cook Time: 10 minutes.
Serves: 4

Ingredients:

- 1/4 cup nutty peanut butter
- 1/4 cup finely diced green onions
- 2 tbsp of soy sauce
- 2 teaspoons lemon juice
- 1 1/2 tbsp. brown sugar
- 2 tbsp. minced garlic
- 1 teaspoon coriander powder
- 1/8 teaspoon cayenne pepper, ground
- 1 pound cubed pork tenderloin 1 (8 ounces) can drained water chestnuts
- 1 medium green bell pepper, diced into 2" bits
- 1 medium red bell pepper, peeled and cut into 2-inch pieces
- skewers, 1 small sweet onion, chopped

Preparation:

1. In a medium mixing bowl, combine peanut butter, green onions, soy sauce, lemon juice, brown sugar, garlic, coriander, and cayenne pepper; stir in pork. Marinate in the refrigerator for at least 30 minutes, covered.

2. Preheat the grill to high. Alternately thread marinated pork, water chestnuts, green bell pepper, red bell pepper, and sweet onion onto skewers. Transfer the remaining marinade to a small saucepan, bring to a boil, and continue to cook for a few minutes.

3. Grates should be lightly oiled. Skewers should be cooked for 10 minutes or until finished to preference. Turn the skewers when grilling to ensure cooking and brush with the boiled marinade in the last few minutes.

Serving Suggestion: Serve over a bed of rice; you can go for sticky rice, jasmine rice, or any other rice appropriate for Thai cuisine or your desired dipping sauce.

Variation Tip: Add Oyster Sauce during or after cooking for an additional flavorful punch.

Nutritional Information Per Serving:

Calories 322 | Fat 16g |Sodium 1015mg | Carbs 23g | Fiber 3g | Sugar 17g | Protein 22g

Thai Waterfall Beef (Waterfall Dish)

Prep Time: 15 minutes.
Cook Time: 12 minutes.
Serves: 4

Ingredients:

- 1 to 2 steaks of sirloin (depending on the amount of meat you prefer)

Marinade:

- 2 tbsp oyster sauce
- 2 tablespoons soy sauce
- 1 tablespoon lime juice (or lemon juice)
- 2 tablespoons brown sugar

Salad Ingredients:

- 6 cups mixed salad greens
- 1 cup sprouted bean
- 1 mint sprig (or basil, fresh, lightly chopped, or torn)
- 1 cup new coriander (fresh)
- 1 papaya cup (fresh, cubed, or cut into spears)
- 1 cup sliced tomatoes (cherry, left whole or sliced in half)

For Dressing:

- 1 to 2 tablespoons fish sauce (available at Asian food stores)
- 3 tablespoons lime juice (or lemon juice)
- 1 1/2 tablespoons soy sauce
- 1 teaspoon cayenne pepper
- 1 teaspoon brown sugar
- 2 tablespoons rice (sticky variety, toasted and ground, OR 2 tbsp. ground peanuts)

Preparation:

1. In a cup or tub, combine the marinade ingredients, stirring to remove the sugar. Pour over the steak(s) and turn to coat. Place in the fridge to marinate.

2. Instead of peanuts, use sticky ground rice: In a dry frying pan over medium-high heat, heat 2 tbsp uncooked sticky rice. Dry-fry the rice, constantly stirring, until it begins to pop and is lightly toasted. Enable the rice to cool slightly before grinding it with a coffee grinder or pounding it into a powder with a pestle and mortar.

3. In a cup or mixing bowl, whisk together all of the dressing ingredients until the sugar dissolves (adjust fish sauce according to your desired level of saltiness). Then, make your salad bowl with greens and other salad ingredients.

4. Grill the steak over a hot grill, rotating just once or twice to keep the juices in the steak (meat should still be pink in the center).

5. If broiling the steak in the oven, preheat the oven to broil. Place the steak on a broiling pan or a baking sheet lined with foil or parchment paper. Preheat the oven to the second-to-highest level. Broil the steak for 5 to 7 minutes per hand, or until it is well cooked on the outside but still pink on the inside.
6. Toss the salad with the dressing while the steak is cooking. Taste for salt, adding more fish sauce if it's not salty enough, or more lime juice if it's too salty.
7. When ready to serve, divide salad among serving plates or bowls. Thinly slice the steak and cover each section with a generous amount of sliced sirloin. Have fun!

Serving Suggestion: Serve over a bed of rice; you can go for sticky rice, jasmine rice, or any other rice appropriate for Thai cuisine.

Variation Tip: Add Banana Blossom/Basil during or after cooking for an additional flavorful punch.

Nutritional Information Per Serving:
Calories 296 | Fat 14g | Sodium 778mg | Carbs 15g | Fiber 3g | Sugar 3g | Protein 29g

Fresh Thai Beef And Peanut Butter Dish

Prep Time: 10 minutes.
Cook Time: 10 minutes.
Serves: 4

Ingredients:

- 1 cup beef stock
- 4 tablespoons peanut butter
- ¼ teaspoon garlic powder
- ¼ teaspoon onion powder
- 1 tablespoon coconut amino
- 1 and ½ teaspoons lemon pepper
- 1 pound beef steak, cut into strips
- Salt and pepper to taste
- 1 green bell pepper, seeded and chopped
- 3 green onions, chopped

Preparation:

1. Take a bowl and add peanut butter, stock, amino, lemon pepper, and stir
2. Keep the mixture on the side
3. Take a pan and place it over medium-high heat
4. Add beef, season with salt, pepper, onion, garlic powder
5. Cook for 7 minutes
6. Add green pepper, stir cook for 3 minutes
7. Add peanut sauce and green onions
8. Stir cook for 1 minute
9. Divide between platters and serve
10. Enjoy!

Serving Suggestion: Serve over a bed of rice; you can go for sticky rice, jasmine rice, or any other rice appropriate for Thai cuisine.

Variation Tip: Add Oyster Sauce during or after cooking for an additional flavorful punch.

Nutritional Information Per Serving:
Calories 219 | Fat 11g | Sodium 450mg | Carbs 14g | Fiber 4g | Sugar 5g | Protein 18g

Thai Mustard Lamb Cutlets

Prep Time: 10 minutes.
Cook Time: 10 minutes.
Serves: 4

Ingredients:

- 2 cups baby spinach, shredded
- 1 cup brown rice, cooked
- 2 cups lamb cutlet, trimmed
- 2 tablespoons white wine vinegar
- 1 tablespoon Dijon mustard
- 1 tablespoon honey 1
- 2 tablespoons Thai curry paste

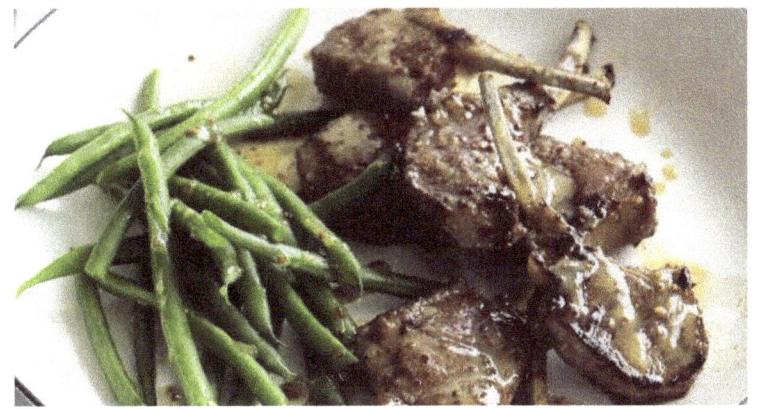

Preparation:

1. Take a pan and place it over medium heat, add coconut oil and warm it
2. Add beef, season with garlic powder, pepper, salt, ginger paste, and onion powder
3. Cook for 4 minutes
4. Mix in broccoli and stir fry for 5 minutes
5. Pour coconut milk, coconut aminos, Thai Curry paste and cook for 15 minutes
6. Serve, sprinkle with cilantro, and sesame seeds
7. Serve and enjoy!

Serving Suggestion: Serve over a bed of rice; you can go for sticky rice, jasmine rice, or any other rice appropriate for Thai cuisine.

Variation Tip: Add Oyster Sauce during or after cooking for an additional flavorful punch.

Nutritional Information Per Serving:
Calories 252 | Fat 21g |Sodium 151mg | Carbs 1g | Fiber 1g | Sugar 0g | Protein 13g

Spiced Beef And Broccoli

Prep Time: 10 minutes.

Cook Time: 15-20 minutes.

Serves: 4

Ingredients:

- ½ cup of coconut milk
- 2 tablespoons coconut oil
- ¼ teaspoon garlic powder
- ¼ teaspoon onion powder
- ½ tablespoon coconut amino
- 1-pound beef steak, cut into strips
- Salt and pepper to taste
- 1 head broccoli, cut into florets
- ½ tablespoon Thai green curry paste
- 1 teaspoon ginger paste
- 1 tablespoon cilantro, chopped
- ½ tablespoon sesame seeds

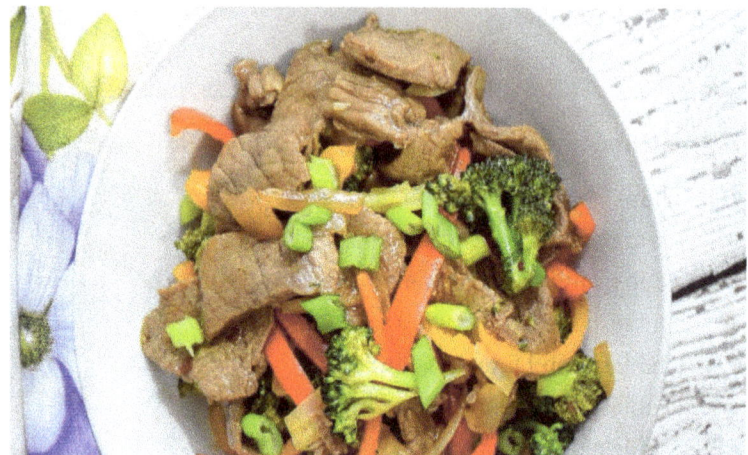

Preparation:

1. Take a pan and place it over medium heat, add coconut oil and warm it
2. Add beef, season with garlic powder, pepper, salt, ginger paste, and onion powder
3. Cook for 4 minutes
4. Mix in broccoli and stir fry for 5 minutes
5. Pour coconut milk, coconut amino, Thai Curry paste and cook for 15 minutes
6. Serve, sprinkle with cilantro, and sesame seeds
7. Serve and enjoy!

Serving Suggestion: Serve over a bed of rice; you can go for sticky rice, jasmine rice, or any other rice appropriate for Thai cuisine.

Variation Tip: Add Chili Peppers/Cilantro/Coriander/Oyster Sauce during or after cooking for an additional flavorful punch.

Nutritional Information Per Serving:

Calories 116 | Fat 10g |Sodium 45mg | Carbs 5g | Fiber 3g | Sugar 1g | Protein 5g

Thai Fried Basil With Pork (Pad Krapow)

Prep Time: 15 minutes.

Cook Time: 10 minutes.

Serves: 4

Ingredients:

- 1-pound ground pork
- 3 tablespoons oil
- 5 minced garlic cloves
- 1 scallion
- 7 chopped green beans
- 2 bird's eye peppers
- 1 teaspoon brown sugar (white sugar is ok too)
- 1 tablespoon fish sauce
- 1 tablespoon medium soy sauce
- 2 tablespoons dark soy sauce (for color)
- 2 tablespoons oyster sauce
- a third of a cup of chicken broth/water
- 1 cup Thai basil (leaves only)
- 1 egg (optional)

Preparation:

1. Cook your garlic and shallots in a big frying pan with vegetable oil over medium-high heat until fragrant and aromatic. After that, add your green beans and bird's eye chili. Cook for a few minutes at a time.

2. Increase the heat to high and add the ground pork, breaking it up to ensure even cooking. Cook until all of the pink is gone.

3. Combine fish sauce, brown sugar, light soy sauce, dark soy sauce, oyster sauce, and chicken broth in a mixing bowl. If the ground pork is cooked, apply this mixture to the pan and continue to cook until the sauce has reduced and the ground pork has caramelized.

4. Finally, add the Thai basil and cook until it begins to wilt. It's now time to eat.

5. Cook your egg in a frying pan over medium-low heat until it is cooked to your liking, then serve on top of the Pad Kra Pao.

Serving Suggestion: Serve over a bed of rice; you can go for sticky rice, jasmine rice, or any other rice appropriate for Thai cuisine. You may opt for Thai Fried Rice as well.

Variation Tip: Add Cilantro/Coriander/Oyster Sauce during or after cooking for an additional flavorful punch.

Nutritional Information Per Serving:

Calories 390 | Fat 29g | Sodium 754mg | Carbs 11g | Fiber 2g | Sugar 5g | Protein 21g

Thai Minced Pork Dish (Laab)

Prep Time: 10 minutes.
Cook Time: 10 minutes.
Serves: 4

Ingredients:

- Canola oil (13 cups)
- 3 tablespoons mashed garlic
- 4 stemmed and minced Thai chiles
- 10 ounces ground pork
- 1 teaspoon crushed red pepper flakes
- 1 teaspoon of Chinese five-spice powder
- 1 tablespoon freshly grated nutmeg
- 1 teaspoon kosher salt
- 14 teaspoon black pepper
- 14 teaspoon ground coriander
- 14 teaspoon ground cardamom
- 2 tablespoons minced mint, plus more for garnish
- 1 tablespoon minced scallions, plus more for garnish
- 1 tablespoon minced cilantro, plus more for garnish
- 2 tablespoons fish sauce
- Garnish with thinly sliced kaffir lime leaves, lemongrass, shallots, cucumbers, and cherry tomatoes.

Preparation:

1. In a 12-inch skillet, heat the oil over medium heat. Cook, constantly stirring, until the garlic and chiles are fragrant, about 2 minutes.
2. Cook, constantly stirring until the pork is browned, about 2 minutes. Add the chile flakes, five-spice, nutmeg, salt, pepper, coriander, and cardamom.
3. Cook until the pork is cooked, about 4 minutes, after adding the mint, scallions, cilantro, and fish sauce.
4. Cover with scallions, cilantro, kaffir leaves, lemongrass, shallots, mint, cilantro, cucumbers, and tomatoes in a large serving dish. At room temperature, serve.

Serving Suggestion: Serve over a bed of rice; you can go for sticky rice, jasmine rice, or any other rice appropriate for Thai cuisine. You may opt for Thai Fried Rice as well.

Variation Tip: Add Oyster Sauce during or after cooking for an additional flavorful punch.

Nutritional Information Per Serving:
Calories 194 | Fat 14g |Sodium 472mg | Carbs 5g | Fiber 2g | Sugar 1g | Protein 12g

Chapter 4: Warm and Desirable Chicken Delights

Tasty Thai Garlic Chicken Breast

Prep Time: 10 minutes.
Cook Time: 25-30 minutes.
Serves: 4

Ingredients:

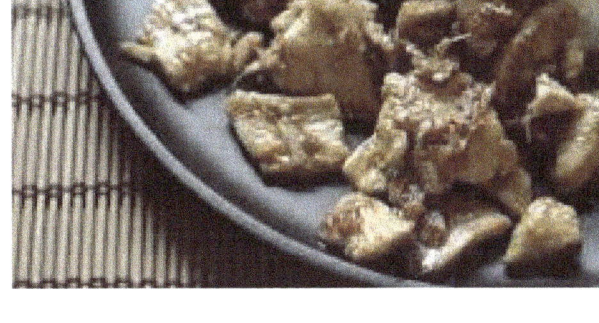

- 1 pound chicken breast tenders
- Cooking spray as needed
- ¼ cup garlic chili sauce
- 2 tablespoons honey
- 1 teaspoon salt
- 1 teaspoon pepper
- 2 cups asparagus spears, chopped
- 1 cup onion, sliced
- 1 tablespoon olive oil
- Cooked rice for serving

Preparation:

1. Pre-heat your oven to 375 degrees F
2. Spray 8x8 baking dish with cooking spray
3. Place chicken in a single layer in a baking dish, season with salt and pepper
4. Take a bowl and add garlic chili sauce, honey, and mix well
5. Pour sauce mixture over chicken, add asparagus and onion
6. Drizzle olive oil
7. Bake for 25-30 minutes
8. Remove from oven and let it rest
9. Enjoy!

Serving Suggestion: Serve over a bed of rice; you can go for sticky rice, jasmine rice, or any other rice appropriate for Thai cuisine. You may opt for Thai Fried Rice as well.

Variation Tip: Add Coriander/Oyster Sauce during or after cooking for an additional flavorful punch.

Nutritional Information Per Serving:

Calories 235 | Fat 17g |Sodium 230mg | Carbs 1g | Fiber 0g | Sugar 0g | Protein 18g

Lovely Fried Chicken (Gai Tod)

Prep Time: 15 minutes.
Cook Time: 10-15 minutes.
Serves: 4

Ingredients:

- 1lb chicken wings
- 1 tbsp coriander seeds, dried
- 1 tablespoon white pepper (substitute black pepper if white pepper is unavailable)
- 4 cloves garlic
- 3 tbsp Thai Soy Sauce (Golden Mountain)
- 1 tablespoon dark Thai soy sauce
- 14 teaspoon salt
- 1 cup of water
- flour made from rice

Preparation:

1. Using a mortar and pestle, pound the dry ingredients (dried coriander seeds, black pepper, white pepper, and garlic cloves) into a paste. A food processor may also be used to make a fast 2-minute marinade.
2. Mix in the wet ingredients (Thai soy sauce, dark soy sauce, salt, and water). Pour marinade sauce over chicken wings and set aside (covered) for several hours, preferably overnight.
3. 4 shallots, thinly sliced, deep-fried until golden and crispy. The shallots will be a garnish for your chicken. Remove the chicken wings from the marinade and dredge in rice flour before frying for 4-6 minutes, or until brown and crispy. For dipping, serve with sticky rice and sweet Thai chili sauce.

Serving Suggestion: Serve over a bed of rice; you can go for sticky rice, jasmine rice, or any other rice appropriate for Thai cuisine. You may opt for Thai Fried Rice as well. You may go for a nice dipping sauce such as Sweet Chili sauce as well.

Variation Tip: Add Banana Blossom/Basil during or after cooking for an additional flavorful punch.

Nutritional Information Per Serving:
Calories 554 | Fat 49g |Sodium 538mg | Carbs 2g | Fiber 0g | Sugar 1g | Protein 25g

Creamy Chicken Coconut Dish (Chicken Khao Soi)

Prep Time: 15 minutes.

Cook Time: 25-30 minutes.

Serves: 4

Ingredients:

- 1 box (6 oz.) chow mein stir-fry noodles
- 1 can (13.5 oz.) coconut milk
- 3/4 cup drained jarred roasted red peppers
- 1 and 1/2 tbsp canola oil
- 3 minced garlic cloves
- 2 shallots, sliced
- 3 tbsp of red curry paste
- 1 1/2 tbsp finely grated ginger
- 2 tablespoons chili powder
- 3 cup chicken broth
- 2 pounds skinless, boneless chicken thighs
- 1 teaspoon fish sauce
- 1 tablespoon low-sodium soy sauce

- 2 tablespoons brown sugar
- 2 tbsp freshly squeezed lime juice

Garnish

- 1/2 tiny thinly sliced red onion
- a half-cup bean sprout
- a half-cup cilantro leaf
- 1 lime (cut into wedges)

Preparation:

1. Cook the noodles according to the package directions; set aside.
2. Blend the coconut milk and red bell peppers until smooth; set aside.
3. In a big stockpot or Dutch oven, heat the canola oil over medium heat. Cook, frequently stirring, until the garlic and shallot are tender, around 3-4 minutes.
4. Stir in the red curry paste, ginger, and chili powder for around 1 minute, or until fragrant.
5. Scrape any browned bits from the bottom of the pot and stir in the chicken stock and coconut milk mixture.
6. Combine the chicken, fish sauce, soy sauce, and brown sugar in a mixing bowl. Bring to a boil; reduce heat and cook, stirring periodically, for 15-20 minutes, or until slightly reduced and chicken is tender.
7. Return the chicken to the pot and shred with two forks; stir in lime juice.
8. Serve immediately with noodles and, if desired, garnished with red onion, bean sprouts, cilantro, and lime.

Serving Suggestion: Serve over a bed of rice; you can go for sticky rice, jasmine rice, or any other rice appropriate for Thai cuisine. You may opt for Thai Fried Rice as well.

Variation Tip: Add Cilantro/Coriander/Oyster Sauce during or after cooking for an additional flavorful punch.

Nutritional Information Per Serving:

Calories 303 | Fat 21g |Sodium 662mg | Carbs 16g | Fiber 1g | Sugar 7g | Protein 15g

Authentic Chicken Fried Rice (Khao Pad)

Prep Time: 15 minutes.
Cook Time: 10-15 minutes.
Serves: 4

Ingredients:

STEP 1 INGREDIENTS

- 1/2 pound thinly sliced chicken
- 1 tbsp Tapioca Flour 1 tbsp Golden Mountain Sauce

STEP 2 INGREDIENTS

- 2 lightly beaten eggs with a pinch of salt
- 1 tsp. finely chopped garlic
- 5 tbsp vegetable oil
- 1 onion, chopped Sliced Coarsely
- 1/4 cup fresh serrano or Thai chile peppers, sliced (seeds removed)
- 6 cups Jasmine rice, cooked (made the day before, left at room temp in rice cooker works best)
- 1 tbsp Golden Mountain Sauce
- 2 tbsp. fish sauce

- 1 1/2 tbsp Roasted Chile Paste (namprik pao)
- a half teaspoon of salt
- 1 teaspoon lime juice
- 1 1/2 Tablespoons Sugar
- 1/2 tsp Thai Pepper Powder
- 1/2 cup Broccoli, cut into small floral florets
- 1 tomato, peeled and cut into wedges
- 2 tablespoons chopped green onion

Preparation:

1. Marinate the chicken in tapioca flour and Golden Mountain sauce for 10 minutes or so.
2. In a wok or skillet, heat 2 tablespoons of oil over medium heat.
3. Allow the eggs to cook before flipping them over and chopping them into smaller pieces with a spatula. Place the egg on a plate and set it aside.
4. Heat the remaining oil in the wok, then add the garlic and cook until golden brown. Stir-fry, the chicken for 3-4 minutes over high heat.
5. Combine the onion, chile pepper, and broccoli in a mixing bowl. Stir all together thoroughly. Pour the next 7 ingredients onto the cooked rice in a separate dish. Add all to the wok gently, stirring carefully to avoid crushing or breaking the rice.
6. Mix all thoroughly. Stir in the tomato, green onion, and egg for about a minute or two. Take the pan off the heat. Garnish with cucumber slices if desired. Have fun!

Serving Suggestion: You may serve with some chicken fry or your desired curry.

Variation Tip: Add Banana Blossom/Oyster Sauce during or after cooking for an additional flavorful punch.

Nutritional Information Per Serving:

Calories 618 | Fat 16g | Sodium 1005mg | Carbs 88g | Fiber 1g | Sugar 8g | Protein 27g

Classic Thick Noodle With Chicken (Pad See Ew)

Prep Time: 15 minutes.
Cook Time: 10 minutes.
Serves: 4

Ingredients:

The Noodle

- 200g dried wide rice stick noodles (7 oz) or 15 oz fresh wide flat rice noodles (450g) (Sen Yai)

APPLE SAUCE

- 2 tablespoons dark soy sauce
- 2 tablespoons oyster sauce
- 2 tablespoons soy sauce (all-purpose or light)
- 2 tablespoons white vinegar (plain white vinegar)
- 2 teaspoons sugar (any type)
- 2 tablespoons water

Stir-Fried

- 3 tbsp divided peanut or vegetable oil
- 2 garlic cloves, very finely chopped 1
- cup / 150g / 5oz boneless, skinless chicken thighs (boneless, skinless), sliced
- 3 tbsp divided peanut or vegetable oil
- 4 Chinese broccoli stems

Preparation:

1. Trim the ends of the Chinese broccoli and cut it into 7.5cm/3-inch bits "fragments Separate the leaves from the roots. Thick stems should be cut in half vertically so that they are no wider than 0.8cm / 0.3 "dense
2. Noodles - Cook and drain according to package instructions. Cook them only before using - if you leave cooked rice noodles lying around, they will break in the wok.
3. Sauce - Combine all of the ingredients in a mixing bowl and whisk until the sugar dissolves.

COOKING:

1. Heat 1 tablespoon oil in a big heavy-bottomed skillet or wok over high heat.
2. Cook for 15 seconds after adding the garlic. Cook until the chicken is mostly white and the color has changed from pink to white.
3. Cook until the chicken is almost finished, then add the Chinese broccoli stems.
4. Cook until the Chinese broccoli leaves are only wilted.
5. Push all to one side, smash an egg into the middle, and scramble. Place all on a plate (scrape wok clean).
6. Return the wok to the stove and heat 2 tablespoons of oil over high heat.

7. Toss in the noodles and sauce. Toss as little as possible to distribute the sauce and caramelize the edges of the noodles.
8. Return the chicken and vegetables to the pan and toss to combine. Serve right away!

Serving Suggestion: You may add some sweet chili sauce to go.

Variation Tip: Add Banana Blossom /Oyster Sauce during or after cooking for an additional flavorful punch.

Nutritional Information Per Serving:

Calories 529 | Fat 7g | Sodium 1386mg | Carbs 94g | Fiber 4g | Sugar 10g | Protein 20g

Perfect Thai Chicken Balls

Prep Time: 15 minutes.
Cook Time: 10 minutes.
Serves: 4

Ingredients:

- 2 pound of ground chicken
- 1 cup of dry bread crumbs
- 4 green onion, sliced
- 1 tablespoon of ground coriander seeds
- 1 cup of fresh cilantro, chopped
- ¼ cup of sweet chili sauce
- 2 tablespoon of fresh lemon juice
- Oil for frying

Preparation:

1. Take a large-sized bowl and add chicken and bread crumbs
2. Mix them well and season with some green onions, cilantro, ground coriander, lemon juice, and chili sauce
3. Mix well
4. Using damp hands, form evenly shaped balls using the mixture
5. Take a large-sized skillet and place it over medium heat
6. Add chicken balls and fry them until all sides are browned up

Serving Suggestion: Serve with your desired dipping sauce, such as Sweet Thai Chili sauce or ketchup.

Variation Tip: Add Banana Blossom/Basil/Chili Peppers/Cilantro/Coriander/Oyster Sauce during or after cooking for an additional flavorful punch.

Nutritional Information Per Serving:
Calories 466 | Fat 20g |Sodium 1272mg | Carbs 34g | Fiber 2g | Sugar 24g | Protein 42g

Fine Chieken Massaman Curry (Matasaman Curry)

Prep Time: 15 minutes.
Cook Time: 35 minutes.
Serves: 4

Ingredients:

- 2 tablespoon of vegetable oil
- 3 tablespoon of curry paste
- 1 sliced and minced ginger
- 1 and a ¼ pound of skinless and boneless chicken breast meat, cubed
- 3 tablespoons of brown sugar
- 3 tablespoon of fish sauce
- 3 tablespoon of tamarind paste
- 1/3 cup of peanut butter
- 3 cups potato, peeled and cubed
- 1 can of coconut milk
- 3 tablespoon of fresh lime juice

Preparation:

1. Take a large-sized saucepan and place it over medium heat
2. Add oil and heat it up
3. Add curry paste and minced ginger, stir fry for 2 minutes
4. Stir in cubed up chicken and cook for about 3 minutes
5. Stir in brown sugar, tamarind sauce, fish sauce, peanut butter, coconut milk, and potatoes
6. Bring it to a boil
7. Lower down the heat to medium-low and simmer for about 20 minutes until the chicken are no longer pink
8. Add lime juice and cook for 5 minutes more
9. Enjoy!

Serving Suggestion: Serve over a bed of rice; you can go for sticky rice, jasmine rice, or any other rice appropriate for Thai cuisine. You may opt for Thai Fried Rice as well.

Variation Tip: Add Banana Blossom during or after cooking for an additional flavorful punch.

Nutritional Information Per Serving:
Calories 682 | Fat 38g |Sodium 1297mg | Carbs 60g | Fiber 9g | Sugar 20g | Protein 33g

Thai Chicken Cashew Meal (Kai Med Ma Muang)

Prep Time: 15 minutes.

Cook Time: 15 minutes.

Serves: 4

Ingredients:

- 1 tablespoon of canola oil
- ¾ cup of cashew nuts
- 15 dried chiles
- 2 roughly chopped garlic cloves
- 1 and a ½ pound of chicken breast cut up into 1-inch pieces
- 5 ounce of quarter button mushrooms
- 3 tablespoon of oyster sauce
- 1 tablespoon of fish sauced
- 1 teaspoon of sugar
- 1 jar of 7 ounces baby corn, drained and halved
- 1 bunch of trimmed scallions cut in 1-inch pieces
- ½ a cup of cilantro leaves
- Cooked jasmine rice

Preparation:

1. Take a wok and place it over medium heat
2. Add oil and heat it up
3. Add cashews, chiles and cook for about 2 minutes
4. Take a slotted spoon and transfer cashews to a bowl
5. Add garlic and to the wok and cook for 1 minute
6. Increase the heat to high and add chicken
7. Cook for 3-5 minutes
8. Add cashews, chiles, and mushrooms, fish sauce, oyster sauce, sugar, corn, spring onion, and cook for 3 minutes until the chicken has been cooked
9. Stir well
10. Serve with some cilantro and over rice

Serving Suggestion: Serve over a bed of rice; you can go for sticky rice, jasmine rice, or any other rice appropriate for Thai cuisine. You may opt for Thai Fried Rice as well.

Variation Tip: Add Banana Blossom /Coriander/Oyster Sauce during or after cooking for an additional flavorful punch.

Nutritional Information Per Serving:

Calories 838 | Fat 58g |Sodium 6064mg | Carbs 23g | Fiber 2g | Sugar 7g | Protein 58g

Thai Pineapple Chicken Curry

Prep Time: 15 minutes.
Cook Time: 35 minutes.
Serves: 4

Ingredients:

- 2 cups of jasmine rice
- 1 quart of water
- ¼ cup of red curry paste
- 2 cans of 13-ounce coconut milk
- 2 skinless and boneless chicken breast halves cut up into thin
- 3 tablespoon of fish sauce
- ¼ cup of white sugar
- 1 and a ½ cups of sliced bamboo shoots
- ½ of red bell pepper, julienned
- ½ of green bell pepper, julienned
- ½ of a small onion, chopped
- 1 cup of pineapple chunks drained up

Preparation:

1. Take a pot of water and bring water to a boil
2. Add rice and lower down the heat to low
3. Simmer for 25 minutes
4. Take a bowl and add the curry paste and 1 can of coconut milk
5. Transfer the mixture to a wok and add the rest of the coconut milk
6. Add chicken, fish sauce, bamboo shoots, and sugar
7. Bring it to a boil and cook further for 1 minute until the chicken juices run clear
8. Take a bowl and mix red bell pepper, onion, and green bell pepper
9. Add to the wok
10. Cook for 10 minutes more until the chicken juices run clear
11. Remove the heat and add pineapple
12. Enjoy!

Serving Suggestion: Serve over a bed of rice; you can go for sticky rice, jasmine rice, or any other rice appropriate for Thai cuisine. You may opt for Thai Fried Rice as well.

Variation Tip: Add /Cilantro/Coriander/Oyster Sauce during or after cooking for an additional flavorful punch.

Nutritional Information Per Serving:
Calories 349 | Fat 27g | Sodium 362mg | Carbs 19g | Fiber 5g | Sugar 6g | Protein 8g

Chicken Satay

Prep Time: 10 minutes.
Cook Time: 5 minutes.
Serves: 4

Ingredients:

- 1 pound of Ground Chicken
- 4 tablespoons of Soy Sauce
- 3 tablespoons of Peanut Butter
- 2 spring onion
- 1/3 Yellow Bell Pepper
- 1 tablespoon of Erythritol
- 1 tablespoon of Rice Vinegar
- 2 teaspoons of Sesame Oil
- 2 teaspoons of Chili Paste
- 1 teaspoon of Minced Garlic
- 1/3 teaspoon of Cayenne Pepper
- ¼ teaspoon of Paprika
- Juice of ½ a lime

Preparation:

1. Heat up about 2 teaspoons of your sesame oil on medium high-heat pan
2. Brown up your chicken and toss in all of the ingredients. Finely mix them and keep cooking
3. Once cooked, toss in about 2 chopped up spring onions and 1/3 of your sliced yellow pepper
4. Serve hot

Serving Suggestion: Serve with your desired dipping sauce, such as Thai sweet chili sauce.

Variation Tip: Add Cilantro/Coriander/Oyster Sauce during or after cooking for an additional flavorful punch.

Nutritional Information Per Serving:

Calories 436 | Fat 15g | Sodium 1605mg | Carbs 5g | Fiber 1g | Sugar 2g | Protein 67g

Chapter 5: Exquisite and Exciting Thai Curries

Authentic Green Curry Prawn

Prep Time: 25 minutes.
Cook Time: 15 minutes.
Serves: 4

Ingredients:

- 1/2 teaspoon cumin powder
- 1 1/2 teaspoon coriander powder
- 1 tbsp fresh ginger root, minced
- 4 tbsp. minced garlic
- 1/3 cup chopped fresh cilantro 2 green chile peppers, chopped 3 stalks lemon grass, minced
- 1 lime, zested 2 limes, juiced
- 2 teaspoons corn oil
- 1/4 cup of corn oil
- 1/2 pound fresh green beans, trimmed 1 (7 ounces) can drained baby corn
- 1 teaspoon soy sauce
- 1 can (14 oz.) coconut milk
- 3/4 pound medium peeled and deveined shrimp (30-40 per pound)

Preparation:

1. In a food processor, combine cumin, coriander, ginger, garlic, green chile peppers, lemon grass, cilantro, lime juice, lime zest, and 2 tablespoons corn oil.
2. To make a smooth, dense paste, combine all of the ingredients in a food processor. Place aside.
3. In a wide skillet over medium-high heat, heat 1/4 cup corn oil. Green beans and baby corn should be cooked and stirred for about 30 seconds.
4. Bring to a boil with the paste, soy sauce, and coconut milk.
5. Reduce the heat to medium and cook for 5 to 7 minutes before adding the shrimp. 3 to 5 minutes, or until the shrimp are bright pink on the outside, and the meat is no longer translucent in the middle.
6. If the sauce becomes too thick, add a splash of water.

Serving Suggestion: Serve over a bed of rice; you can go for sticky rice, jasmine rice, or any other rice appropriate for Thai cuisine. You may opt for Thai Fried Rice as well.

Variation Tip: Add Banana Blossom during or after cooking for an additional flavorful punch.

Nutritional Information Per Serving:

Calories 400 | Fat 31g |Sodium 727mg | Carbs 13g | Fiber 2g | Sugar 3g | Protein 21g

Thai Monkfish Curry

Prep Time: 20 minutes.
Cook Time: 20 minutes.
Serves: 4

Ingredients:

- 1 teaspoon of peanut oil
- 12 finely chopped sweet onion
- 1 chopped red bell pepper
- 3 tbsp. red Thai curry paste
- 1 can (14 oz.) coconut milk
- 12 ounces monkfish, cubed
- 1 teaspoon fish sauce
- 2 teaspoons lime juice
- 2 tbsp. cilantro, chopped

Preparation:

1. In a large sauce pan over medium heat, heat the peanut oil. Cook until the onion is softened and translucent, 3 to 5 minutes. Cook for 3 to 5 minutes more, or until red bell pepper is softened. Cook for 1 minute after adding the curry paste. Pour in the coconut milk and bring to a gentle simmer.
2. When the coconut milk starts to boil, add the cubed monkfish and cook for 7 to 10 minutes, or until the fish is firm and the middle is no longer opaque. Until serving, combine the fish sauce, lime juice, and cilantro.

Serving Suggestion: Serve over a bed of rice; you can go for sticky rice, jasmine rice, or any other rice appropriate for Thai cuisine. You may opt for Thai Fried Rice as well.

Variation Tip: Add Chili Peppers/Cilantro/Coriander/Oyster Sauce during or after cooking for an additional flavorful punch.

Nutritional Information Per Serving:
Calories 593 | Fat 22g |Sodium 2010mg | Carbs 29g | Fiber 4g | Sugar 4g | Protein 68g

Thai Potato Yellow Curry

Prep Time: 15 minutes.
Cook Time: 25 minutes.
Serves: 4

Ingredients:

- 1 tablespoon olive oil
- ½ a yellow onion, sliced
- 1 pound boneless skinless chicken breasts, diced
- 3 tablespoons yellow curry paste
- 10 baby golden Yukon potatoes, peeled and diced

- 1 14-ounce can coconut cream (similar to coconut milk, but much more decadent)
- 1 – 1/2 cup water
- 2 tablespoons fish sauce (optional)
- 1/2–1/4 tbsp brown sugar (optional)

Preparation:

1. In a large pot, heat the oil over medium-low heat. Sauté the onions for a few minutes, or until they are fragrant and softened. Cook for 3-5 minutes after adding the chicken and curry paste. Stir in the potatoes to coat with the curry paste.
2. Add the coconut cream and 1/2 cup water to the pot and lower down heat, simmer for 20-30 minutes, Until the chicken and potatoes are completely cooked, adding more water as required to achieve the desired sauce consistency.
3. To kick it up a notch, add the fish sauce and brown sugar. Seriously, it's fantastic. Serve with rice.

Serving Suggestion: Serve over a bed of rice; you can go for sticky rice, jasmine rice, or any other rice appropriate for Thai cuisine. You may opt for Thai Fried Rice as well.

Variation Tip: Add Coriander/Oyster Sauce during or after cooking for an additional flavorful punch.

Nutritional Information Per Serving:
Calories 286 | Fat 11g | Sodium 161mg | Carbs 35g | Fiber 13g | Sugar 18g | Protein 17g

Pork Red Curry With Squash (Gaeng Daeng Sai Fak Thong Lae Moo)

Prep Time: 15 minutes.
Cook Time: 25 minutes.
Serves: 2

Ingredients:

- 1 Tbsp. vegetable oil
- 1 tbsp red curry paste (or to taste)
- 12 pound thinly sliced pork loin
- 1 can (14 oz.) coconut milk
- 2 1/4 cup butternut squash, peeled and cubed
- 2 1/4 cup coarsely chopped cabbage
- 1 tbsp fish sauce (or more to taste)
- 1 tbsp white sugar (or more to taste)

Preparation:

1. In a medium pot, heat the oil over medium heat. Stir in the curry paste for 2 to 3 minutes, or until fragrant. Pork should be included.
2. 3 to 5 minutes more, stir-fry until cooked through and coated in curry paste. Bring the coconut milk to a gentle boil. Squash should be included.
3. Reduce heat to low and cook until squash is just tender, 7 to 10 minutes.
4. Cook for 5 minutes more after adding the cabbage. Season with fish sauce and sugar to taste.

Serving Suggestion: Serve over a bed of rice; you can go for sticky rice, jasmine rice, or any other rice appropriate for Thai cuisine. You may opt for Thai Fried Rice as well.

Variation Tip: Add Banana Blossom/ Coriander/Oyster Sauce during or after cooking for an additional flavorful punch.

Nutritional Information Per Serving:
Calories 536 | Fat 41g |Sodium 1251mg | Carbs 17g | Fiber 5g | Sugar 4g | Protein 31g

Traditional Coconut Shrimp Curry

Prep Time: 15 minutes.
Cook Time: 120 minutes.
Serves: 4

Ingredients:

- 1 pound shrimp, with shells
- 3 and ¾ cups light coconut milk
- 1 and ¾ cups water
- ½ cup Thai Red curry sauce
- 2 and ½ teaspoons lemon garlic seasoning
- ¼ cup cilantro

Preparation:

1. Add coconut milk, red curry sauce, water, lemon garlic seasoning, and cilantro to your Slow Cooker
2. Give it a nice stir
3. Cook on HIGH for 2 hours
4. Add shrimp and cook for another 15-30 minutes
5. Garnish with some cilantro and serve!

Serving Suggestion: Serve over a bed of rice; you can go for sticky rice, jasmine rice, or any other rice appropriate for Thai cuisine. You may opt for Thai Fried Rice as well.

Variation Tip: Add Banana Blossom/Basil/Chili Peppers during or after cooking for an additional flavorful punch.

Nutritional Information Per Serving:

Calories 239 | Fat 17g | Sodium 653mg | Carbs 7g | Fiber 1g | Sugar 2g | Protein 17g

Thai Broccoli And Chickpea Curry

Prep Time: 15 minutes.
Cook Time: 15 minutes.
Serves: 4

Ingredients:

- 2 tablespoons cooking oil
- 2 garlic cloves, minced
- ¼ cup Thai red curry paste
- 2 heads broccoli, cut into florets
- 15 ounces/425 grams of coconut milk
- 14 ounces/396 grams chickpeas, drained and rinsed
- 1 tablespoon cornstarch, dissolved in 1/4 cup cold water

Preparation:

1. Build a campfire by arranging a bed of coal and letting the fire burn until coals are red hot, 12 coals on bottom
2. Place Dutch Oven over hot coal, add garlic, and cook for 3 minutes
3. Stir in curry paste, cook for 1 minute
4. Add broccoli and cook for 2-3 minutes
5. Add coconut milk, cook for 3 minutes
6. Add chickpeas, bring back to boil
7. Stir in cornstarch mixture and cook well for 2 minutes more
8. Once the sauce is thick, serve and enjoy!

For stovetop cooking, the required temperature (approximately) is 325 Degrees F /160 Degrees C. For a 10-inch Dutch Oven

Serving Suggestion: Serve over a bed of rice; you can go for sticky rice, jasmine rice, or any other rice appropriate for Thai cuisine. You may opt for Thai Fried Rice as well.

Variation Tip: Add Banana Blossom/Basil/Chili Peppers during or after cooking for an additional flavorful punch.

Nutritional Information Per Serving:

Calories 321 | Fat 20g |Sodium 179mg | Carbs 29g | Fiber 5g | Sugar 7g | Protein 10g

Authentic Green Curry (Gaeng Keow Wan Gai)

Prep Time: 15 minutes.
Cook Time: 40-50 minutes.
Serves: 4

Ingredients:

- 3-pound frying boneless skinless chicken cut into tiny chunks
- 4 c. coconut milk
- 2 teaspoons fish sauce
- 3 tsp Laos powder
- 3 tbsp. green curry paste (see my recipe)
- 1/2 cup sweet basil leaves, new
- 8 lime leaves, young and new
- 1/2 cup fresh green peas
- 7 serrano peppers

Preparation:

1. In a wok or big frying pan, combine the chicken, 2 cups of coconut milk, fish sauce, and Laos powder, and bring to a boil, cooking until the chicken is cooked and tender.
2. With a slotted spoon, remove your chicken from the pan, leaving everything else behind, and place it on a plate to set aside.
3. Allow the milk to boil until it is very thick and "oily."
4. After that, apply your curry paste to the pan.
5. Allow for 3 minutes of cooking time, or until all is smooth and even.
6. Return the chicken to the pan, pour in the remaining coconut milk, and bring the whole mixture to a boil.
7. Reduce the heat to low and leave it to cook for about 10 minutes.
8. Finally, add your basil and citrus leaves, peas, and serranos, and bring to a boil for 5 minutes.
9. Serve right away.

Serving Suggestion: Serve over a bed of rice; you can go for sticky rice, jasmine rice, or any other rice appropriate for Thai cuisine. You may opt for Thai Fried Rice as well.

Variation Tip: Add Chili Peppers/Cilantro/Coriander/Oyster Sauce during or after cooking for an additional flavorful punch.

Nutritional Information Per Serving:

Calories 3225 | Fat 26g |Sodium 722mg | Carbs 10g | Fiber 1g | Sugar 1g | Protein 16g

Curried Coconut Chicken

Prep Time: 15 minutes.
Cook Time: 50 minutes.
Serves: 4

Ingredients:

- 2 pounds of chicken breast, cut up into ½ inch chunks
- 1 teaspoon of pepper and salt
- 1 and a ½ tablespoon of vegetable oil
- 2 tablespoon of curry powder
- ½ of an onion, thinly sliced
- 2 crushed garlic cloves
- 1 can of 14-ounce coconut milk
- 1 can of 14.5 ounces can of stewed diced tomatoes
- 1 can of 8-ounce tomato sauce
- 3 tablespoons of sugar

Preparation:

1. Season your chicken with pepper and salt
2. Take a large-sized skillet and heat up some oil over medium-high heat
3. Add the curry powder and stir cook for 2 minutes
4. Stir in your onions and garlic and cook for another minute
5. Add your chicken, making sure to toss it well, and coat it up with the curry oil
6. Lower down the heat to medium and cook the chicken for about 10 minutes
7. Pour the coconut milk, tomato sauce, tomatoes, sugar into your pan and stir everything to combine it well
8. Cover it up and simmer it for about 40 minutes
9. Serve!

Serving Suggestion: Serve over a bed of rice; you can go for sticky rice, jasmine rice, or any other rice appropriate for Thai cuisine. You may opt for Thai Fried Rice as well.

Variation Tip: Add Banana Blossom/Cilantro/Coriander/Oyster Sauce during or after cooking for an additional flavorful punch.

Nutritional Information Per Serving:

Calories 300 | Fat 24g |Sodium 342mg | Carbs 8g | Fiber 2g | Sugar 2g | Protein 14g

Exciting Peanut Shrimp Curry

Prep Time: 15 minutes.
Cook Time: 10 minutes.
Serves: 4

Ingredients:
- 2 tablespoon of Green Curry paste
- 1 cup of vegetable stock
- 1 cup of coconut milk
- 6 ounces of Pre-Cooked shrimp
- 5 ounce of Broccoli florets
- 3 tablespoons of chopped Cilantro
- 2 tablespoons of Coconut Oil
- 1 tablespoon of Peanut Butter
- 1 tablespoon of Soy Sauce
- ½ of a lime juice
- 1 medium-sized spring onion chopped up
- 1 teaspoon of crushed roasted garlic
- 1 teaspoon of minced garlic

- 1 teaspoon of fish sauce
- ½ teaspoon of Turmeric
- ¼ teaspoon of Xanthan Gum
- ½ of a cup of source cream

Preparation:
1. Startup by taking a pan over medium heat and add up 2 tablespoons of coconut oil
2. Once the oil is melted, toss in the minced ginger and chopped up spring onion. Let them cook for about a minute before pouring the turmeric and curry paste
3. Add about 1 tablespoon of soy sauce, peanut butter, and fish sauce and mix them well
4. Then add in a cup of vegetable stock and just a cup of coconut milk.
5. Stir them well before adding the green curry paste.
6. Simmer them for a while
7. Add about ¼ teaspoon of Xanthan Gum to the curry and mix it properly
8. After a while, you will notice that the curry will begin to thicken; that will be the moment when you are going to be needing to throw in the florets and stir them finely
9. Add in the fresh chopped cilantro
10. Once the consistency is fine, you are going to need to toss the weighed pre-cooked shrimp and add the lime juice
11. Let the mixture for a few minutes and season it with pepper and salt as required
12. Finally, serve it hot alongside just a ¼ a cup of sour cream with each serving

Serving Suggestion: Serve over a bed of rice; you can go for sticky rice, jasmine rice, or any other rice appropriate for Thai cuisine. You may opt for Thai Fried Rice as well.

Variation Tip: Add Banana Blossom/Basil/Chili Peppers/Cilantro during or after cooking for an additional flavorful punch.

Nutritional Information Per Serving:
Calories 329 | Fat 28g |Sodium 593mg | Carbs 16g | Fiber 2g | Sugar 3g | Protein 8g

Panang Curry

Prep Time: 10 minutes.
Cook Time: 15 minutes.
Serves: 4

Ingredients:

- 2 tablespoons of vegetable oil
- boneless chicken thighs 14 oz (cut into small pieces)
- 1/2 cup red bell pepper, sliced
- 1/2 cup yellow bell pepper, sliced
- 1 cup broccoli florets
- 4 tbsp Panang curry paste
- 1 tbsp coconut sugar
- 5 to 6 Kaffir lime leaves (chopped)
- 2 red bird's eye chilies (chopped)
- 2 quarts of coconut milk
- 1 cup water, seasoned to taste
- 2 tablespoons sauce of fish
- 1 bunch Thai basil

Preparation:

1. Begin by chopping the chicken and vegetables. 14 oz boneless chicken breast, washed and cut into 1-inch cubes with a sharp knife 12 red bell peppers, 12 yellow bell peppers, and a small broccoli head cut into bite-size florets
2. In a medium-sized pan, heat 2 tbsp vegetable oil.
3. Fry the chicken pieces in the pan on high heat for 3-4 minutes or until they are slightly browned.
4. Note: If making vegan, omit this phase. You may substitute another kind of meat for the chicken.
5. Fry for 2 minutes with 12 cup sliced red bell peppers, 12 cup sliced yellow bell peppers, and 1 cup tiny broccoli florets.
6. Please keep in mind that you can use any vegetables you want.
7. Place the chicken and vegetables on the pan's side.
8. To the pan, add 4 tbsp Panang curry paste.
9. Note: For a vegan version, use vegan Panang curry paste instead of the standard one, which contains shrimp paste. If you prefer a milder curry, reduce the amount of paste used.
10. Fry for 2 minutes before mixing it together.
11. Cook for another minute after adding 1 tbsp palm sugar.
12. Allow the curry to simmer for 10-12 minutes after adding 5-6 sliced Kaffir lime leaves, 2 chopped bird's eye red chilies, and 2 cups coconut milk. Now, add 1 cup of water and thoroughly combine.
13. Mix in 2 tbsp fish sauce and a pinch of broken Thai basil.
14. To make it vegan, omit the fish sauce and replace it with soy sauce or tamari.

15. Serve immediately.

Serving Suggestion: Serve over a bed of rice; you can go for sticky rice, jasmine rice, or any other rice appropriate for Thai cuisine. You may opt for Thai Fried Rice as well.

Variation Tip: Add Banana Blossom/Basil during or after cooking for an additional flavorful punch.

Nutritional Information Per Serving:

Calories 516 | Fat 31g |Sodium 1405mg | Carbs 15g | Fiber 1g | Sugar 7g | Protein 45g

Chapter 6: Inspiring Thai Veggie Delights

Stir-Fried Baby Mushrooms

Prep Time: 10 minutes.
Cook Time: 15 minutes.
Serves: 4

Ingredients:

- 2 tablespoons olive oil
- 3 garlic cloves, minced
- 1 onion, diced
- 8 baby corn ears, sliced
- 2/3 pound fresh mushrooms, sliced
- 1 tablespoon fish sauce
- 1 tbsp. mild soy sauce
- 1 teaspoon oyster sauce
- 2 tablespoons cornstarch
- 3 tbsp water
- 1/4 cup chopped fresh cilantro 1 red chile pepper, sliced

Preparation:

1. In a large skillet or wok, heat the oil over medium heat; cook the garlic in the hot oil until browned, 5 to 7 minutes.
2. Cook until the onion and baby corn are translucent, around 5 to 7 minutes. Cook the mushrooms in the mixture for around 2 minutes or until they are slightly softened.
3. Stir in the fish sauce, soy sauce, and oyster sauce until thoroughly combined.
4. In a small cup, whisk together the cornstarch and water until the cornstarch is dissolved; pour into the mushroom mixture.
5. Cook, constantly stirring until the sauce is thickened and glistening.
6. To eat, move to a serving dish and garnish with chile pepper and cilantro.

Serving Suggestion: Serve with some Sweet Thai Chili Sauce or your desired dipping sauce.

Variation Tip: Add Banana Blossom/Basil/Chili Peppers/ Coriander/Oyster Sauce during or after cooking for an additional flavorful punch.

Nutritional Information Per Serving:

Calories 223 | Fat 8g |Sodium 286mg | Carbs 34g | Fiber 3g | Sugar 5g | Protein 6g

Stir-Fried Bok Choy And Sesame

Prep Time: 10 minutes.
Cook Time: 15 minutes.
Serves: 4

Ingredients:

- 2 large bunch bok choy, cut off, leaves rinsed
- 1 tablespoon sesame oil
- 1 tablespoon olive oil
- 2 whole eggs
- 2 tablespoons low-carb soy sauce
- 1 tablespoon sesame seeds

Preparation:

1. Take a frying pan and place it over medium heat.
2. When the pan is hot, add the sesame seeds and toast till it turns golden.
3. Add olive oil, sesame oil, and soy sauce, then bring to a simmer.
4. Add the bok choy and stir to coat in oil and soy sauce.
5. Stir the bok choy continuously as it cooks and wilts.
6. Once done, remove it from the pan and set it aside.
7. Add egg replacers to the pan.
8. Scramble them in the remaining soy sauce and oil till just set.
9. Spoon the scrambled eggs over the bok choy.
10. Serve and enjoy.

Serving Suggestion: Serve over a bed of rice; you can go for sticky rice, jasmine rice, or any other rice appropriate for Thai cuisine. You may opt for Thai Fried Rice as well.

Variation Tip: Add Banana Blossom/ Oyster Sauce during or after cooking for an additional flavorful punch.

Nutritional Information Per Serving:

Calories 114 | Fat 9g |Sodium 558mg | Carbs 10g | Fiber 3g | Sugar 4g | Protein 3g

Cool Stir-Fried Vegetable (Pad Pak Ruammit)

Prep Time: 15 minutes.
Cook Time: 10-15 minutes.
Serves: 4

Ingredients:

- a half-cup broccoli
- 1/2 cup vegetables
- 1 cup of baby corn
- 1/2 cup carrots, sliced
- 1/2 cup red pepper, sliced
- 1/2 cup white mushrooms, sliced
- 1 garlic clove, finely chopped
- 1/2 cup sugar
- 1 tablespoon soy sauce
- 2 tablespoons oyster sauce
- 2 tablespoons water
- 2 tablespoons sesame oil

Preparation:

1. First, we'll make the stir fry sauce. In a mixing bowl, combine 2 tbsp oyster sauce, 1/2 tbsp sugar, 1 tbsp soy sauce, and 2 tbsp water.
2. Heat 2 tablespoons of sesame oil in a wok over high heat, then add 1 clove finely chopped garlic and 1/2 cup sliced carrots and stir fry for 1 minute.
3. To the wok, add 1/2 cup broccoli, 1/2 cup baby corn, and 1/2 cup mange tout and stir fry for another minute or so.
4. Add 1/2 cup sliced red peppers and 1/2 cup sliced white mushrooms, followed by the sauce we made earlier. Stir all together for a few minutes more, until the vegetables are cooked to your taste, then serve with steamed jasmine rice!

Serving Suggestion: Serve over a bed of rice; you can go for sticky rice, jasmine rice, or any other rice appropriate for Thai cuisine. You may opt for Thai Fried Rice as well.

Variation Tip: Add Banana Blossom/Basil/Chili Peppers/Cilantro/Coriander/Oyster Sauce during or after cooking for an additional flavorful punch.

Nutritional Information Per Serving:
Calories 170 | Fat 15g | Sodium 133mg | Carbs 7g | Fiber 1g | Sugar 3g | Protein 4g

Lovely Morning Glory Stir Fry (Pad Pak Boong)

Prep Time: 10 minutes.
Cook Time: 2-3 minutes.
Serves: 4

Ingredients:

- 1 pound Morning Glory
- 2-3 Thai chili peppers, new (Or 2 small dried chili peppers)
- 6 garlic cloves

Stir-Fry Sauce

- 1 tbsp Korean Soybean Paste (Doenjang) (Miso Paste is also acceptable!)
- 1 teaspoon Mirim (Rice Wine)
- 1 tbsp Oyster Sauce
- 1/2 tbsp. Soy sauce
- ½ tablespoon sugar

Additional Ingredient for Stir-Frying

- 1/2 Tablespoon Soy Sauce
- 3-4 Tablespoons Cooking Oil
- a pinch of water

Preparation:

Preparation Ingredients

1. Clean Morning Glory thoroughly. Set it in a strainer and let the excess water drain. The stems should then be cut into pinky-finger lengths. Then, cut the leafy part into pointer-finger lengths
2. Remove the garlic cloves' ends. Then get out your mortar and pestle. Pound the garlic cloves (6) and chili peppers (2-3) together gently. After that, set aside.
3. Stir together the following ingredients to make the Stir-fry Sauce: Soybean Paste (1 Tablespoon), Mirim (1 Tablespoon), Oyster Sauce (1 Tablespoon), Soy Sauce (1/2 Tablespoon), and Sugar (1/2 Tablespoon). Thoroughly combine all of the ingredients.

Preparing the Meal

1. In a wok or frying pan, heat 3-4 tablespoons cooking oil. Plan on cooking on medium-high heat. When the oil is hot, add the garlic and chili peppers first.
2. Stir-fry until the mixture becomes aromatic. Then add the stems of morning glory. 1/2 Tablespoon Soy Sauce comes next. For 30 seconds, stir-fry the stems in the soy sauce.
3. Add the leaves after 30 seconds. Then whisk in the rest of the stir-fry sauce.
4. Stir-fry for another 15-20 seconds. Remove from heat and place on a tray.
5. Serve right away with a bowl of hot rice!

Serving Suggestion: Serve over a bed of rice; you can go for sticky rice, jasmine rice, or any other rice appropriate for Thai cuisine. You may opt for Thai Fried Rice as well.

Variation Tip: Add Banana Blossom/Basil/Chili Peppers/Cilantro during or after cooking for an additional flavorful punch.

Nutritional Information Per Serving:

Calories 301 | Fat 22g | Sodium 661mg | Carbs 14g | Fiber 5g | Sugar 7g | Protein 19g

Thai Stir-Fried Pumpkin Meal (Pad Fuk Thong)

Prep Time: 10 minutes.
Cook Time: 5-10 minutes.
Serves: 4

Ingredients:

- 2 tablespoons olive oil
- 1 tsp. finely chopped garlic
- 1 Cup Pork, Finely Chopped (or other meat or tofu)
- 1 1/2 cup (bite-size) Peeled pumpkin cubes
- 2 beaten eggs
- 1 tablespoon Oyster Sauce (vegetarian if desired)
- 1 tbsp. light soy sauce
- 1 tsp Golden Mountain Seasoning Sauce
- 1 Tablespoon Sugar
- 1/4 cup stock (chicken or vegetable)
- a half-cup Green onion, 2 inches long

Preparation:

1. In a wok, heat the oil until it is very hot. Stir in the garlic and cook until golden brown. Cook until the meat or tofu is finished.
2. Combine the pumpkin, stock, oyster sauce, soy sauce, seasoning sauce, and sugar in a mixing bowl.
3. Stir all together and cook for 3 minutes, or until the pumpkin is almost cooked.
4. Break the eggs into the wok and stir to combine; add the green onion and remove from the heat.
5. Serve with freshly steamed jasmine rice.

Serving Suggestion: Serve over a bed of rice; you can go for sticky rice, jasmine rice, or any other rice appropriate for Thai cuisine. You may opt for Thai Fried Rice as well.

Variation Tip: Add Banana Blossom/Basil/Chili Peppers/Cilantro/Coriander during or after cooking for an additional flavorful punch.

Nutritional Information Per Serving:
Calories 365 | Fat 26g |Sodium 490mg | Carbs 23g | Fiber 4g | Sugar 5g | Protein 11g

Awesome Thai Banana Custard

Prep Time: 15 minutes.

Cook Time: 60 minutes.

Serves: 4

Ingredients:

- 1 cup of coconut milk
- 1/3 cup of sugar
- 2 whole egg
- 1 ripe banana
- 1 teaspoon of coconut flavoring
- Oil for grease

Preparation:

1. Pre-heat your oven to a temperature of 350 degrees Fahrenheit
2. Prepare 4-6 ramekins and grease them up with a bit of oil
3. Add your coconut milk, eggs, sugar, banana, and flavorings into a blender and mix well for 30 seconds
4. Pour the mixture into your ramekins, making sure to fill them up by 3/4rth
5. Add the ramekins to a flat-bottomed glass dish and fill the dish partway with water (about ½ the height of your ramekins)
6. Bake for about 60 minutes until a nice custardy texture appears
7. Serve your ramekins hot or chilled
8. If needed, then sprinkle a bit of sugar or shredded coconut on top

Serving Suggestion: Serve with a topping of ice cream for more taste

Variation Tip: Add some shredded coconut on top

Nutritional Information Per Serving:

Calories 243 | Fat 6g | Sodium 162mg | Carbs 42g | Fiber 3g | Sugar 24g | Protein 8g

Delicious Mango Rice Pudding (Kao Niew Ma Muang)

Prep Time: 15 minutes.
Cook Time: 5 minutes.
Serves: 4

Ingredients:

- 2 medium mangos
- 3 teaspoons gelatin
- ½ cup hot water
- 1/3 cup white sugar
- 1 cup coconut milk

Preparation:

1. Scoop out the flesh off your Mangoes fruit and place them in a food processor
2. Blitz them until a mango puree form
3. Leave it be
4. Take a saucepan and place it over medium heat
5. Add water and allow it to heat up
6. Remove the heat and keep stirring it while adding the gelatin to the surface
7. Stir well to ensure that no lumps are formed
8. Add sugar to the water/gelatin mix and stir well
9. Add the mixture to your mango puree
10. Add coconut milk
11. Blitz well until the ingredients are combined well
12. Pour the mixture into your dessert bowls
13. Allow them to chill for 2 hours
14. Serve with some fresh fruit!

Serving Suggestion: Serve with a topping of Ice Cream for added flavor!

Variation Tip: Add some shredded coconut on top

Nutritional Information Per Serving:

Calories 789 | Fat 30g | Sodium 1346mg | Carbs 123g | Fiber 4g | Sugar 71g | Protein 7g

A Fruity Bowl

Prep Time: 15 minutes.

Cook Time: Nil.

Serves: 4

Ingredients:

- 2 fresh ripe mangoes
- 2 cups of pineapple chunks
- Fresh pineapple tips
- 1 sliced banana
- 1-2 cups of fresh papaya slice up into cubes
- Kiwi fruits sliced up into cubes
- Dragon fruits sliced up into cubes
- 2 cups of fresh seedless grapes sliced up in half
- ¼ cup of coconut milk
- 2 tablespoon of lime juice
- 3-4 tablespoon of sugar (depending on your preference)

Preparation:

1. Slice up the listed fruits except for the contrasting red ones (raspberries, dried cranberries, and strawberries) and add them to a mixing bowl
2. Drizzle a bit of lime juice on top and stir well
3. Sprinkle some sugar and stir well
4. Chill in your fridge for 30 minutes
5. Before serving the salad, add a bit of coconut milk and give the mixture a stir
6. Taste it and adjust the sweetness accordingly
7. Top it up with some raspberries, dried cranberries, and strawberries
8. Serve!

Serving Suggestion: Serve with a topping of Ice Cream!

Variation Tip: Add some shredded coconut on top

Nutritional Information Per Serving:

Calories 260 | Fat 1g | Sodium 30mg | Carbs 66g | Fiber 4g | Sugar 59g | Protein 2g

Hearty Banana Fries

Prep Time: 15 minutes.
Cook Time: 15 minutes.
Serves: 4

Ingredients:

- ¾ cup of white rice flour
- ¼ cup of tapioca flour
- 2 tablespoons of white sugar
- 1 teaspoon of salt
- ½ a cup of shredded coconut
- 1 and a ¼ cups of water
- 10 bananas, sliced
- 3 cups of oil for frying

Preparation:

1. Take a medium-sized bowl and add rice flour, salt, coconut, and tapioca
2. Mix well
3. Stir in water a bit at a time and keep mixing it until a thick batter form
4. Peel the bananas and cut them into lengthwise 3-4 pieces
5. Take a deep fryer and add oil, and allow it to heat up
6. Coat the banana slices in the batter and fry them until golden
7. Allow them to drain on a kitchen towel, serve and enjoy!

Serving Suggestion: Serve with a topping of Ice Cream for extra flavor; you may drizzle a bit of chocolate syrup as well.

Variation Tip: Add some shredded coconut on top!

Nutritional Information Per Serving:

Calories 200 | Fat 10g |Sodium 119mg | Carbs 28g | Fiber 1g | Sugar 12g | Protein 3g

Green Papaya Mix (Som Tum)

Prep Time: 15 minutes.
Cook Time: Nil.
Serves: 4

Ingredients:

- 10 small-sized dried shrimp
- 2 small-sized red Thai chiles
- 1 peeled garlic clove
- ¼ cup of tamarind juice
- 1 tablespoon of grated palm sugar
- 1 tablespoon of Thai fish sauce
- 1 lime cut up into 1-inch pieces
- 4 cherry tomatoes, halved
- 3 long beans, trimmed up into 1-inch pieces
- 1 carrot, shredded
- ½ of an English cucumber coarsely and seeded
- 1/6 of small green cabbage, cored and thinly sliced
- 1 pound of unripe green papaya, quartered seeded, and finely shredded using a mandolin
- 3 tablespoons of unsalted roasted peanuts

Preparation:

1. Take a mortar and pestle and crush your shrimp alongside garlic, chiles
2. Add tamarind juice, fish sauce, and palm sugar
3. Squeeze 3 quarts of lime pieces over the mortar
4. Grind to make a dressing
5. Add the remaining ingredients (excluding the peanut), making sure to add the papaya last
6. Use the pestle and spoon to grind well
7. Mix the vegetable and fruit and coat them well
8. Transfer to your serving dish
9. Garnish with some peanuts and lime pieces
10. Enjoy!

Serving Suggestion: Serve over a bed of rice; you can go for sticky rice, jasmine rice, or any other rice appropriate for Thai cuisine. You may opt for Thai Fried Rice as well.

Variation Tip: Add Banana Blossom/Basil /Oyster Sauce during or after cooking for an additional flavorful punch.

Nutritional Information Per Serving:

Calories 132 | Fat 3g |Sodium 1445mg | Carbs 27g | Fiber 6g | Sugar 16g | Protein 4g

Chapter 7: Amazing Rice Companions

Awesome Ginger Chicken With Jasmine Rice

Prep Time: 35 minutes.
Cook Time: 40 minutes.
Serves: 4

Ingredients:

- 1 cup jasmine rice, uncooked
- 1/4 teaspoon turmeric powder
- 1 1/4 pound skinless, boneless chicken breast halves, cut into thin strips
- 3 tablespoons canola oil
- 1 small eggplant, quartered lengthwise, then crosswise into 1/2-inch-thick slices
- 1 large red bell pepper, sliced into 2-inch strips
- 1 large onion, cut in half and thinly sliced into 1/2-inch slices
- 1/4 cup Swanson® Thai Ginger Flavor Infused Broth 2 minced garlic cloves
- 3/4 cup coconut milk (unsweetened)
- 2 seeded and chopped jalapeno peppers
- 1 cup cilantro leaves, fresh

Preparation:

1. Cook the rice according to package directions, adding the turmeric to the cooking water halfway through.
2. In a 12-inch skillet, heat 1 tablespoon oil over medium-high heat. Cook, frequently stirring until the chicken is browned. Take the chicken out of the skillet.
3. In the skillet, heat the remaining oil. Cook, occasionally stirring, for 5 minutes, or until the eggplant, red pepper, and onion are tender-crisp. Cook and stir for 1 minute after adding the garlic. Bring the broth to a boil, then remove it from the heat. Turn the heat down to medium. Cook, occasionally stirring, for 8 minutes.
4. In a blender, combine the coconut milk, jalapeno peppers, and cilantro. Blend until the mixture is smooth, then cover and set aside.
5. In the skillet, stir the coconut milk mixture. Put the chicken back in the skillet. Cook until the chicken is thoroughly cooked. Serve the chicken and rice mixture together.

Serving Suggestion: You may consider some dipping sauce such as soy sauce or Chili Sauce.

Variation Tip: Add Coriander/Oyster Sauce during or after cooking for an additional flavorful punch.

Nutritional Information Per Serving:

Calories 760 | Fat 35g |Sodium 2005mg | Carbs 62g | Fiber 1g | Sugar 18g | Protein 47g

Original Thai Omelet (Kai Jeow)

Prep Time: 10 minutes.
Cook Time: 5 minutes.
Serves: 4

Ingredients:

- two eggs
- a half teaspoon of fish sauce
- 2 sliced green onions
- 1 Tbsp. vegetable oil

Preparation:

1. Green onions, thinly sliced in a mixing bowl, combine the eggs and fish sauce until frothy. Stir in the green onions.
2. In a small nonstick skillet, heat the oil over medium heat until it is very hot. Cook until the egg mixture is browned and crispy on the one hand, around 1-2 minutes.
3. Cook for another 1-2 minutes, or until the other side is browned, but the inside is still fluffy. (If you don't feel comfortable flipping the omelet all at once, fold it in half after about a minute and brown on both sides.)
4. If desired, serve with steamed jasmine rice and sriracha sauce.

Serving Suggestion: Serve over a bed of rice; you can go for sticky rice, jasmine rice, or any other rice appropriate for Thai cuisine. You may opt for Thai Fried Rice as well.

Variation Tip: Add Banana Blossom/Basil/Oyster Sauce during or after cooking for an additional flavorful punch.

Nutritional Information Per Serving:

Calories 208 | Fat 15g | Sodium 347mg | Carbs 6g | Fiber 1g | Sugar 3g | Protein 12g

Traditional Thai Rice Pudding

Prep Time: 15 minutes.
Cook Time: 15 minutes.
Serves: 4

Ingredients:

- 2 cups of Thai sweet rice (known as sticky or glutinous rice)
- 3 and a ½ cup of water
- ½ a teaspoon of salt
- 1 can of coconut milk
- ¾ cup of palm sugar
- 1 teaspoon of vanilla
- 1 teaspoon of cinnamon
- 1/4 teaspoon of nutmeg
- ¼ teaspoon of ground cloves

Preparation:

1. Take a large-sized pot with a lid and add 2 cups of water
2. Add the rice and let it soak for about 10 minutes
3. Add 1 and a ½ cups of water and salt
4. Stir well
5. Place the mixture over high heat and bring it to a boil
6. Lower the heat to medium-low just as it starts to boil and partially cover the pot with a lid
7. Boil it as such for 15-20 minutes until the water has been absorbed
8. Remove the heat and let the rice steam for 10 minutes (by keeping the lid on)
9. Remove the lid and add coconut milk and keep stirring well until fully mixed
10. Turn the heat to low and simmer it
11. Add ¾ cup of sugar
12. Add vanilla, nutmeg, cinnamon, and cloves
13. Taste it for sweetness and season to your preference
14. Eventually, the rice will absorb the coconut milk and turn into a nice rice pudding
15. Garnish with some cinnamon, crushed peanuts, star anise, and serve!

Serving Suggestion: Serve with a topping of ice cream if desired.

Variation Tip: Add Banana Blossom/Basil/Oyster Sauce during or after cooking for an additional flavorful punch.

Nutritional Information Per Serving:

Calories 135 | Fat 5g |Sodium 84mg | Carbs 20g | Fiber 1g | Sugar 1g | Protein 4g

Sweet And Spicy Coconut Mango Rice

Prep Time: 60 minutes.
Cook Time: 10 minutes.
Serves: 4

Ingredients:

- 1 cup of sticky rice
- 1 and a ¾ cup of water
- 1 can of coconut milk
- 2 cups of white sugar
- 1 pinch of salt
- 2 teaspoon of corn starch dissolved in 2 tablespoons of water
- 2 ripe mangoes cut up into bite-sized portions
- 1 cup of sticky rice
- 1 and a ¾ cup of water
- 1 can of coconut milk
- 2 cups of white sugar
- 1 pinch of salt
- 2 teaspoon of corn starch dissolved in 2 tablespoons of water
- 2 ripe mangoes cut up into bite-sized portions

Preparation:

1. Soak the sticky rice in 1 cup of water and allow them to soak for about 60 minutes
2. Add ¾ cup of water to the rice and bring it to a boil over high heat
3. Lower down the heat to low and cover with a lid
4. Take a saucepan and add ¾ cup of coconut cream and place it over medium heat
5. Allow it to simmer while adding sugar, keep stirring it until the sugar dissolves fully
6. Once the rice is ready, pour the coconut sauce onto the sticky rice
7. Remove the heat and cover with your lid for about 15 minutes
8. Pour ¼ cup of coconut cream into the saucepan and allow it to simmer with salt and cornstarch
9. Assemble on a serving platter by adding the mango pieces, sticky rice and pour over the coconut cream
10. Enjoy!

Serving Suggestion: Serve with a topping of Ice Cream if desired.

Variation Tip: Add Chili Peppers/Cilantro/ during or after cooking for an additional flavorful punch.

Nutritional Information Per Serving:

Calories 789 | Fat 30g |Sodium 1346mg | Carbs 127g | Fiber 4g | Sugar 4g | Protein 7g

Coconut Black Beans

Prep Time: 15 minutes.
Cook Time: 10 minutes.
Serves: 4

Ingredients:

- 1 cup coconut milk
- ½ cup palm sugar
- ½ teaspoon salt
- Water as needed
- ½ cup black beans

Preparation:

1. Soak your black beans overnight under 2 cups of water (the key is to ensure that the water level is 2 inches higher than the beans)
2. Take a pot of water and bring it to a boil
3. Add the beans and boil them for about 25 minutes until they are soft
4. Remove the heat
5. Drain them and reserve the bean water
6. Take another pot and add coconut milk, salt, and palm sugar
7. Bring the mix to a simmer and keep stirring it constantly to prevent over-boiling
8. Once the coconut milk starts to look white /yellowish, let it simmer for another 2-4 minutes
9. Add the beans to the coconut milk and add 1 cup of your bean water
10. Let it boil again and wait until the milk shows a purple color
11. Let it boil again and check for sweetness
12. Serve when done!

Serving Suggestion: Serve with a topping of Ice Cream in addition to the flavor.

Variation Tip: Add some shredded coconut on top for more flavor

Nutritional Information Per Serving:

Calories 429 | Fat 23g |Sodium 622mg | Carbs 44g | Fiber 17g | Sugar 3g | Protein 15g

Tom Yum Fried Rice with Shrimp (Khao Pad Tom Yum)

Prep Time: 10 minutes.

Cook Time: 5 minutes.

Serves: 4

Ingredients:

- 30 wonton wrappers
- 1 pound peeled, deveined, tail-on raw shrimp (about 30)
- Neutral oil, such as peanut or refined coconut oil, for frying
- Sweet Chili Sauce

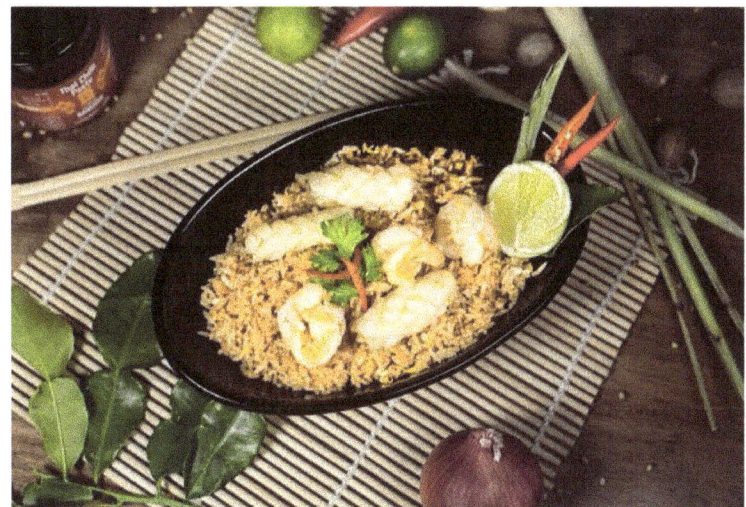

Preparation:

1. Clean your work surface and place the wrappers.
2. Use your finger to straighten out each shrimp a bit and place it at the edge of one of the wrappers, leaving the tail off the wrapper.
3. Bring the remaining wrapper all the way over to cover the shrimp.
4. Then, use your thumbs to grab the edge on which the shrimp is lying and roll up to form a cylinder.
5. Use water at the tip of your finger to seal the wrapper.
6. Take a deep skillet over medium-high heat, heat 1 inch of oil to 375 degrees F
7. Fry the rolls in batches
8. Be careful not to overcrowd them, just until crisp and golden brown, 1 to 2 minutes.
9. Drain well on paper towels and serve with chili sauce for dipping.
10. Serve and enjoy!

Serving Suggestion: Serve over a bed of rice; you can go for sticky rice, jasmine rice, or any other rice appropriate for Thai cuisine. You may opt for Thai Fried Rice as well.

Variation Tip: Add Banana Blossom/Oyster Sauce during or after cooking for an additional flavorful punch.

Nutritional Information Per Serving:

Calories 182 | Fat 6g | Sodium 436mg | Carbs 24g | Fiber 1g | Sugar 0g | Protein 7g

Green Curry Fried Rice (Khao Pad Gaeng Kiew Wan)

Prep Time: 5 minutes.
Cook Time: 5 minutes.
Serves: 4

Ingredients:

- 4 ounces of any boneless meat (such as pork or chicken), cut against the grain into thin, bite-size pieces (about ¼ inch by 2 to 3 inches)
- ½ cup green peas, fresh or frozen
- 2 cups cooked rice, at room temperature (preferably day-old)
- 2 tablespoons Green Curry Paste
- 2 tablespoons vegetable oil
- 1 tablespoon water, if needed
- 2 teaspoons fish sauce
- 1 teaspoon palm sugar or granulated sugar
- 2 fresh kaffir lime leaves, center ribs removed and julienned, optional
- 1 cup fresh Thai sweet or Italian sweet basil leaves, optional

Preparation:

1. Take a large skillet over medium heat.
2. Heat the oil.
3. Add the curry paste and stir-fry until fragrant for about 1 minute.
4. Add the water if needed, fish sauce, and sugar.
5. Stir-fry until the sugar dissolves, about 30 seconds.
6. Add the meat and peas, and stir-fry until the meat is no longer pink for 3 to 4 minutes.
7. Add the rice and kaffir lime leaves and stir-fry for about 1 minute.
8. Turn off the heat and stir in the basil leaves just until wilted.
9. Serve immediately and enjoy!

Serving Suggestion: Serve over a bed of rice; you can go for sticky rice, jasmine rice, or any other rice appropriate for Thai cuisine.

Variation Tip: Add Banana Blossom/Basil/Chili Peppers during or after cooking for an additional flavorful punch.

Nutritional Information Per Serving:
Calories 495 | Fat 7g | Sodium 1605mg | Carbs 101g | Fiber 10g | Sugar 29g | Protein 13g

Pineapple Fried Rice with Curry Powder and Shrimp (Khao Pad Sapparot)

Prep Time: 10 minutes.
Cook Time: 5 minutes.
Serves: 4

Ingredients:

- 10 medium raw shrimp, peeled and deveined, tails left on
- 2 cups cooked rice, at room temperature (preferably day-old)
- 2 teaspoons curry powder
- 1 egg
- 2 teaspoons fish sauce
- 2 tablespoons vegetable oil
- 1 tablespoon garlic, minced
- ½ cup cashew nuts, roasted
- ¼ cup onion, very thinly sliced
- 2 lime wedges
- 1 cup fresh pineapple, 1-inch chunks
- 2 scallions, cut into ¼-inch slices
- 1 tablespoon soy sauce
- 2 tablespoons fresh cilantro leaves
- Pinch sugar, granulated

Preparation:

1. Take a small bowl and add soy sauce, fish sauce, curry powder, and sugar.
2. Mix them well and keep them aside.
3. Take a large skillet and add oil, then place it over medium heat.
4. Add the garlic and stir-fry until fragrant, 30 seconds to 1 minute.
5. Then add the onion.
6. Cook until fragrant and the onion is softened for about 30 seconds.
7. Crack the egg into the center of the wok or skillet
8. Stir with a wooden spoon or spatula to mix the egg and yolk well, about 30 seconds.
9. Add the rice, and stir-fry until it is evenly mixed with the egg, about 1 minute.
10. Add the sauce mixture, cashews, scallions, and pineapple.
11. Stir-fry for 30 seconds longer.
12. Add sprinkled with cilantro and with lime wedges for squeezing over each portion.
13. Serve and enjoy!

Serving Suggestion: Serve over a bed of rice; you can go for sticky rice, jasmine rice, or any other rice appropriate for Thai cuisine. You may opt for Thai Fried Rice as well.

Variation Tip: Add Banana Blossom/ Oyster Sauce during or after cooking for an additional flavorful punch.

Nutritional Information Per Serving:

Calories 207 | Fat 3g | Sodium 406mg | Carbs 46g | Fiber 3g | Sugar 38g | Protein 3g

Coconut Rice (Khao Mun Gati)

Prep Time: 5 minutes.

Cook Time: 15 minutes.

Serves: 4

Ingredients:

- 2 cups jasmine rice, uncooked
- 1 cup coconut milk
- ½ teaspoon salt
- 1 and ¾ cups water

Preparation:

1. Rinse the rice well.
2. Take a medium pot and add water, coconut milk, and salt
3. Place it over medium heat until the salt dissolves.
4. Transfer the rice to the pot.
5. Stir a few times and bring to a boil.
6. Cover the pot and reduce the heat to the lowest setting, and simmer
7. Keep heating until most of the coconut milk is absorbed for about 15 minutes.
8. Don't open the pot or stir the rice while it's cooking.
9. Remove from the heat, stir a few times with a fork or spatula
10. Serve and enjoy!

Serving Suggestion: Serve over a bed of rice; you can go for sticky rice, jasmine rice, or any other rice appropriate for Thai cuisine. You may opt for Thai Fried Rice as well.

Variation Tip: Add Banana Blossom/Basil during or after cooking for an additional flavorful punch.

Nutritional Information Per Serving:

Calories 554 | Fat 32g | Sodium 429mg | Carbs 59g | Fiber 3g | Sugar 1g | Protein 8g

Fresh Spring Rolls (Poh Piah Sod)

Prep Time: 15 minutes.
Cook Time: 10 minutes.
Serves: 4

Ingredients:

- 3 ounces rice-vermicelli noodles, thin
- 8 round, dried rice paper spring roll sheets
- 8 shrimp, cooked, peeled, and halved lengthwise
- ½ cup carrot, grated
- ½ cup bean sprouts
- ¼ cup fresh mint leaves
- ¼ cup fresh cilantro leaves
- 2 or 3 scallions, green parts only, cut into 4-inch lengths

Preparation:

1. Take a small pot to add water so that it covers the vermicelli noodles.
2. Cover it and bring it to a boil over high heat.
3. Plunge the noodles into the boiling water to cover.
4. Then take them off the heat and set them for 6 to 8 minutes.
5. Rinse them well in cold running water and set them aside.
6. Arrange all ingredients in small bowls, then fill a shallow pan with very hot water.
7. Dip each rice paper sheet into the hot water and turn it in a circular motion.
8. Shake off any excess water.
9. Take a large plate or tray, then place the softened rice sheet into it.
10. Place 2 shrimp halves, pink-side down in the middle of the lower third of the sheet.
11. Arrange about ¼ cup of the vermicelli noodles in a cylindrical shape on top of the shrimp.
12. Add bean sprouts and carrots on top of the noodles.
13. Then 3 or 4 mint leaves and 3 or 4 cilantro leaves, and then one of the scallion sections.
14. Roll the rice sheets from the bottom up and tucking them tightly around the filling.
15. Halfway rolled, firmly fold in the left and right sides of the sheet to form an envelope shape.
16. Keep rolling, and then place the finished roll on the tray seam-side down.
17. Let it dry for 5 to 10 minutes before you serve.
18. Serve and enjoy!

Serving Suggestion: Serve with your desired dipping sauce. You may go for garlic sauce, soy sauce, Thai sweet Chili Sauce, and so on.

Variation Tip: Add Banana Blossom/Basil /Oyster Sauce during or after cooking for an additional flavorful punch.

Nutritional Information Per Serving:
Calories 136 | Fat 3g |Sodium 756mg | Carbs 24g | Fiber 3g | Sugar 10g | Protein 3g

Chapter 8: Beautiful Noodle Based Recipes

The Original Noodle Soup (Guawy Teow)

Prep Time: 15 minutes.
Cook Time: 20 minutes.
Serves: 4

Ingredients:

- 500 g (1 pound) fresh big rice noodle
- 2 tablespoons lard (or vegetable oil)
- 2 tbsp divided vegetable oil
- 10 shelled and deveined tiny prawns/shrimp
- 2 finely chopped garlic cloves
- 1 Chinese sausage / Lup Chong Sausage, thinly sliced on the diagonal 5 cm / 2"-piece fried fish cake, thinly sliced
- 20 garlic chives leaves, sliced into 4 sections
- 2 and ½ cup bean sprouts
- 2 whisked eggs

THE SAUCE:

- 5 tablespoons dark soy sauce
- 4 tsp mild soy sauce
- 2 tablespoons oyster sauce
- 4 tablespoons kecap Manis (sweet soy sauce)

Preparation:

1. Combine sauce ingredients well
2. Do not try to pull noodles apart when they are cold and hard; they may split.
3. Place the entire packet in the microwave and heat on high for 1 1/2 to 2 minutes, or until warm and pliable but not hot, turning the packet over as required.
4. Handle with care and position 500g/1-pound noodles in a heatproof dish. Noodles that have been trapped together must be separated.
5. If the noodles become cold and brittle before cooking, cover with cling wrap and microwave for 30 seconds (not hot, just warm) to avoid breakage.
6. In a large nonstick skillet, heat 1 tablespoon oil over high heat.
7. When the pan is hot, add the shrimp and cook for 1 1/2 minutes, or until just cooked through, before transferring to a bowl.
8. Cook for 1 minute, or until the Chinese sausage and fish cake are caramelized, before adding to the dish.

9. Cook, pressing in the edges to create a dense omelet with 1 tbsp oil. Once it's set, roughly chop it with a wooden spoon (as seen in the video), then add it to the cup.
10. Cook for about 1 minute, or until the bean sprouts begin to wilt, before adding to the bowl.
11. Pour in the lard. When the butter has melted and begins to smoke, add the garlic and immediately add the noodles. Fold gently four times with a spatula and a wooden spoon (as seen in the video) to distribute the oil in the noodles.
12. Return all of the other ingredients, including the chives, to the pot. Fold gently twice more, then pour over the whole amount of Sauce.
13. Gently toss 4 to 6 times to distribute the sauce, pausing in between to allow the noodles to caramelize on the edges a little.
14. Remove from the heat and serve right away.

Serving Suggestion: Serve with some sweet chili sauce or soy sauce.

Variation Tip: Add Banana Blossom/Basil/Chili Peppers/Cilantro during or after cooking for an additional flavorful punch.

Nutritional Information Per Serving:
Calories 902 | Fat 56g | Sodium 1455mg | Carbs 29g | Fiber 4g | Sugar 5g | Protein 68g

Thai Peanut Butter Noodles

Prep Time: 15 minutes.

Cook Time: 10 minutes.

Serves: 4

Ingredients:

- ½ a cup of chicken broth
- 1 and a ½ tablespoon of minced fresh ginger root
- 3 tablespoon of soy sauce
- 1 and a ½ tablespoon of honey
- 2 teaspoons of hot chile paste
- 3 garlic cloves, minced
- 8 ounce of Udon noodles
- ¼ cup green onions, chopped
- ¼ cup peanuts, chopped

Preparation:

1. Take a large-sized pot and add water
2. Bring it to a boil and add noodles and cook them until they are soft
3. Drain the noodles
4. Take a small saucepan and add chicken broth, soy sauce, ginger, peanut butter, chili paste, honey, and garlic
5. Cook it over medium heat until the peanut butter has fully melted
6. Add noodles and give it a toss
7. Garnish it with peanuts and onions
8. Serve!

Serving Suggestion: Serve with some sweet chili sauce or soy sauce.

Variation Tip: Add Banana Blossom/Basil/Oyster Sauce during or after cooking for an additional flavorful punch.

Nutritional Information Per Serving:

Calories 436 | Fat 16g | Sodium 36mg | Carbs 57g | Fiber 7g | Sugar 7g | Protein 20g

Sukothai Pad Thai

Prep Time: 15 minutes.
Cook Time: 20 minutes.
Serves: 4

Ingredients:

- ½ a cup of white sugar
- ½ a cup of distilled vinegar
- ¼ cup of soy sauce
- 2 tablespoon of tamarind sauce
- 1 pack of 12 ounces dried rice noodles
- ½ a cup of vegetable oil
- 1 and a ½ teaspoon of minced garlic
- 4 pieces of eggs
- 1 pack of 12-ounce firm tofu cut up into ½ inch strips
- 1 and a ½ tablespoon of white sugar
- 1 and ½ teaspoon of salt
- 1 and a ½ cups of ground peanuts

- 1 and a ½ teaspoon of ground dried oriental radish
- ½ a cup of chopped fresh chives
- 1 tablespoon of paprika
- 2 cups of fresh bean sprouts
- 1 lime cut up into wedges

Preparation:

1. Take a saucepan and place it over medium heat
2. Add sugar, vinegar, soy sauce, and tamarind pulp and blend them well
3. This is your Pad Thai sauce
4. Soak noodles under cold water until they are tender
5. Take a large-sized skillet and place it over medium heat
6. Add oil and warm it
7. Add garlic and eggs, cook and scramble the egg
8. Add tofu and stir well until mixed
9. Add noodles and stir cook
10. Stir in Pad Thai sauce, 1 and a ½ teaspoon of salt, and 1 and a ½ tablespoon of sugar
11. Stir in peanuts and ground radish
12. Remove the heat and add paprika and chives
13. Stir for a while and serve with bean sprouts and lime

Serving Suggestion: Serve with some sweet chili sauce or soy sauce.

Variation Tip: Add Banana Blossom/Basil/Chili Peppers during or after cooking for an additional flavorful punch.

Nutritional Information Per Serving:

Calories 260 | Fat 30g |Sodium 1345mg | Carbs 75g | Fiber 3g | Sugar 15g | Protein 16g

Thai-Style Stir-Fried Macaroni (Pad Macaroni)

Prep Time: 10 minutes.
Cook Time: 15 to 20 minutes.
Serves: 4

Ingredients:

- 9 ounces chicken breast, pork, or shrimp cut into bite-size pieces
- 3 scallions, cut into 2-inch lengths, white parts also halved lengthwise, kept separate
- 9 ounces macaroni
- 3 tablespoons ketchup
- ½ carrot, peeled and cut crosswise into thin slices
- 2 garlic cloves, finely minced
- 1 onion, cut into ¼ -inch slices
- 1 to 2 tablespoons Sriracha sauce
- 1 large egg
- 2 tomatoes, cored and each cut into 8 wedges
- 1 tablespoon soy sauce
- 2 teaspoons fish sauce
- 2 tablespoons vegetable oil
- Ground white pepper for serving

Preparation:

1. Take a large pot of water over high heat to boil for the pasta.
2. When the water reaches a rolling boil, and adds a pinch of salt and the pasta.
3. Cook the pasta until just about 1 minute short of al dente.
4. Drain well, rinse in cold running water, and set aside.
5. Take a small bowl and add ketchup, Sriracha, soy sauce, and fish sauce.
6. Mix them well and set them aside.
7. Take a large skillet over high heat, then heat the oil until shimmering.
8. Add the garlic and stir-fry until lightly golden for 30 seconds to 1 minute.
9. Add the onion and carrot, and continue to stir-fry until the vegetables are softened.
10. Cook for 2 to 3 minutes.
11. Add the chicken and scallion whites and continue stir-frying until the meat is browned
12. Then the scallion whites are softened for 3 to 4 minutes.
13. Push all the ingredients to the sides of the wok or skillet with a wooden spoon.
14. Break the egg into the middle of the skillet and lightly scramble it for about 30 seconds.
15. Add the cooked pasta and sauce and toss everything well.
16. Add the tomatoes and scallion greens and continue stir-frying for about 1 minute.

17. Add a sprinkle of white pepper on top.
18. Serve and enjoy!

Serving Suggestion: Serve with some sweet chili sauce or soy sauce.

Variation Tip: Add Banana Blossom/Basil/Chili Peppers/Cilantro/Coriander/Oyster Sauce during or after cooking for an additional flavorful punch.

Nutritional Information Per Serving:

Calories 774 | Fat 38g |Sodium 1530mg | Carbs 57g | Fiber 3g | Sugar 10g | Protein 51g

Pad Thai

Prep Time: 10 minutes.
Cook Time: 10 minutes.
Serves: 4

Ingredients:

- 12 medium raw shrimp, peeled and deveined, tails left on
- 4 ounces thin rice noodles, dried
- 2 eggs
- 2 cups bean sprouts, divided
- 3 tablespoons palm sugar, light brown sugar, or granulated sugar
- 3 scallions, green parts only, cut into 1 and ½ -inch lengths
- ¼ cup fish sauce
- 2 tablespoons shallot, minced
- 1 tablespoon garlic, minced
- 1 to 2 tablespoons water or broth, if needed
- ½ cup pressed tofu or bean curd, cut into ¼ -inch by ¼ -inch by 2-inch slices
- ¼ cup roasted peanuts plus more for serving, slightly crushed in a mortar and pestle or roughly chopped
- 2 tablespoons tamarind paste
- 3 tablespoons vegetable oil, divided
- Lime wedges, for serving

Preparation:

1. Take a large pot of water to boil over high heat.
2. When boiling, turn off the heat.
3. Add the noodles, then stir a few times and let sit for 5 minutes.
4. Rinse the noodles well under cold water and drain well.
5. Use your finger to separate them.
6. Take a small bowl and add fish sauce, palm sugar, and tamarind paste.
7. Mix them well and set them aside.
8. Take a large skillet over medium heat.
9. Heat 1 tablespoon of oil.
10. Add the shrimp and stir-fry just until pink and opaque, 2 to 3 minutes.
11. Remove the shrimp from the wok or skillet with a mesh skimmer or slotted spoon and set aside.
12. Heat the remaining 2 tablespoons of oil in the skillet and add the shallot and garlic.
13. Stir-fry until fragrant and slightly golden, 30 seconds to 1 minute.
14. Add the noodles and sauce mixture, and stir-fry until well-combined and the noodles are soft but not mushy about 1 minute.
15. Add 1 to 2 tablespoons water or broth if the noodles are not soft enough.

16. Push the noodles to the sides of the wok or skillet with a wooden spoon or spatula.
17. Crack the eggs into the middle of the wok or skillet, and scramble with a wooden spoon just until nearly set, about 30 seconds.
18. Add the cooked shrimp, 1 cup bean sprouts, and the tofu, scallions, and peanuts, and toss to combine.
19. Add the lime wedges, the remaining 1 cup bean sprouts, and additional peanuts to sprinkle on top.
20. Serve and enjoy!

Serving Suggestion: Serve with some sweet chili sauce or soy sauce.

Variation Tip: Add Banana Blossom/Oyster Sauce during or after cooking for an additional flavorful punch.

Nutritional Information Per Serving:

Calories 748 | Fat 23g |Sodium 689mg | Carbs 95g | Fiber 5g | Sugar 4g | Protein 32g

Chapter 9: Refreshing Drinks

Refreshing Thai Iced Tea (Cha Yen)

Prep Time: 15 minutes.
Cook Time: 1 minute.
Serves: 1

Ingredients:

- 1 tbsp Thai black tea
- 1 cup hot, scalding water
- 2 tsp condensed milk, sweetened
- 2 tbsp evaporated milk (plus some more to sprinkle on top)
- 2 tsp sugar
- 1 cup ice, crushed

Preparation:

1. The first step is to bring water to a boil; I'm only using a kettle, but you might also use a water boiler or microwave.
2. Fill your tea sock with 1 tablespoon of Thai black tea. It is easiest to place your tea sock in a bowl or large cup to steep the tea.
3. Pour 1 cup of boiling water into the tea sock and gently force it in and out to steep the tea and absorb all of the flavors. Steep the tea for a few minutes or until it has turned a pleasant dark color.
4. Pour 1 glass of hot tea into a fresh cup.
5. Stir in 2 teaspoons of sugar and 2 teaspoons of sweetened condensed milk.
6. Then whisk in 2 teaspoons of evaporated milk, continuing to stir until all is thoroughly combined.
7. Optional - A good Thai iced tea should have some froth or bubbles on top, so take two pitchers and spill the tea from one to the other with a bit of elevation. You might do it differently, but it's a lot of fun!
8. Fill a cup all the way to the top with crushed ice.
9. The gentry Pour your hot tea mixture over the ice in a cup.
10. Drizzle some more evaporated milk on top of your Thai iced tea to add a final creamy touch.
11. With the addition of a straw, you're able to slurp it down!

Serving Suggestion: Serve chilled with some ice cubes if you want it to be more refreshing.

Variation Tip: Add some shredded coconut on top

Nutritional Information Per Serving:

Calories 186 | Fat 0g | Sodium 16mg | Carbs 48g | Fiber 2g | Sugar 43g | Protein 1g

Lovely Pink Milk (Thai Nom Yen)

Prep Time: 5 minutes.
Cook Time: Nil
Serves: 4

Ingredients:

- 1 tablespoon sala syrup
- 2 tablespoons condensed milk
- 3/4 cup of milk
- 8 optional ice cubes

Preparation:

1. Take a sizable bottle. For an extra chilled experience, place it in the freezer for 5-10 minutes before serving. After that, fill it with ice (optional).
2. Combine the sala syrup and condensed milk in a mixing bowl.
3. Pour in your milk, stir all together, and serve right away.

Serving Suggestion: Serve chilled with some ice cubes if you want it to be more refreshing.

Variation Tip: Add some shredded coconut on top

Nutritional Information Per Serving:

Calories 174 | Fat 12g |Sodium 43mg | Carbs 16g | Fiber 0g | Sugar 4g | Protein 2g

Awesome Thai Bubble Tea (Boba Tea)

Prep Time: 5 minutes.
Cook Time: 5 minutes
Serves: 1

Ingredients:

TO MAKE THE THAI TEA:

- 13 cup (180 ml) Pantai Thai Tea Blend
- 3 quarts (720 mL) of water

FOR THE BOBA & COMPLETING THE DRINK:

- 1/2 cup (100 g) granulated sugar
- half a cup (120 ml) tapioca pearls that have been dried
- 1/2 cup (120 mL) milk, half-and-half, or another creamer (some people use coconut milk, heavy cream, or sweetened condensed milk)

Preparation:

1. Bring the water to a boil before adding the Thai tea mix and sugar. Stir until the sugar is fully dissolved. Tea should be gently boiled for about 3 minutes. Take the pan off the heat.
2. Enable the tea to steep for at least 30 minutes before serving. The stronger the tea flavor, the better Thai tea tastes.
3. Set aside the Thai tea to cool (we prefer to strain through a traditional re-useable cloth filter to remove any sediment). You can make this ahead of time and store the Thai tea in the refrigerator. Chill completely before serving.
4. Cook tapioca pearls according to package directions; see Note 1 for instructions on cooking the boba we purchased.
5. Divide the warm tapioca pearls into two (16-ounce) glasses. Fill the two glasses halfway with cold tea.
6. Fill with glass with around 1/4 cup milk (or preferred creamer). Enjoy with a straw after you've stirred it up.

Serving Suggestion: Serve chilled with some ice cubes if you want it to be more refreshing.

Variation Tip: Add some shredded coconut on top

Nutritional Information Per Serving:

Calories 449 | Fat 1g | Sodium 49mg | Carbs 111g | Fiber 1g | Sugar 75g | Protein 0g

Simple Lemongrass Drink

Prep Time: 10 minutes.
Cook Time: 10 minutes
Serves: 1

Ingredients:

- 5 big lemongrass stalks
- 2 and 1/2 cup water
- 1/4–1/2 cup sugar
- Pinch of salt
- Lime Juice

Preparation:

1. Thinly slice the lemongrass.
2. Simmer for 7-8 minutes in a saucepan with the water.
3. Stir in the sugar to dissolve it. Allow cooling before straining the lemongrass.
4. Serve over a large amount of ice.

Serving Suggestion: Serve chilled with some ice cubes if you want it to be more refreshing.

Variation Tip: Add some shredded coconut on top!

Nutritional Information Per Serving:

Calories 395 | Fat 4g | Sodium 37mg | Carbs 95g | Fiber 20g | Sugar 66g | Protein 7g

Authentic Iced Coffee (Oliang)

Prep Time: 15 minutes.
Cook Time: Nil
Serves: 4

Ingredients:

- 2 tbsp Oliang powder
- 300ml of water
- 3 heaping tablespoons sugar
- 3 tbsp sweetened condensed milk (sweetened)
- ice, crushed

Preparation:

1. Fill the muslin filter halfway with Oliang powder.
2. Bring water to a boil and slowly pour it through the muslin filter into a clean tub.
3. Pour the liquid two more times through the same muslin filter.
4. The coffee is ready when all of the liquid has been drained from the filter for the third time.
5. Stir in the sugar and condensed milk until the sugar dissolves.
6. Place the mixture in the freezer for about 15 minutes to cool.
7. Pour the coffee into a tumbler over crushed ice, leaving space for milk or cream on top.

Serving Suggestion: Serve chilled with some ice cubes if you want it to be more refreshing.

Variation Tip: Add some shredded coconut on top!

Nutritional Information Per Serving:

Calories 446 | Fat 26g | Sodium 162mg | Carbs 49g | Fiber 0g | Sugar 36g | Protein 5g

Conclusion

Thailand is the most acclaimed nation in the whole world for its cooking. Traversing from the southern landmass toward the northern regions, the nation offers a varied mix of madly flavorful food. Thai food is not the only cuisine to have been changed in the excursion across seas. Various vegetarian Thai foods are loved across the world. You, in particular, would enjoy cooking your vegetarian food with the Thai flavors inserted in them.

The different flavours utilized in Thai cooking have a tremendous measure of astounding properties that soundly affect our general wellbeing. This cookbook incorporates 80 healthy Thai recipes covering poultry, snacks, noodle, curries, salads, seafood, and everything in between that you can undoubtedly make at home without the help of any kind.

I would like to thank you for purchasing and downloading my book. I really do hope that you had a pleasant time with my book and enjoyed reading it.

I bid you farewell and hope that your journey into the world of Thai cuisine may turn out to be a huge success! I Stay healthy and stay safe.

www.ingramcontent.com/pod-product-compliance
Lightning Source LLC
Chambersburg PA
CBHW080608170426
43209CB00007B/1367